THEOPOLITAN LITURGY

THEOPOLIS FUNDAMENTALS
SERIES INTRODUCTION

The Theopolis Institute is a community of pastors, theologians, and students devoted to articulating and disseminating a vision of the church's mission to contemporary culture, a vision that centers on biblical theology and liturgical practice. The church carries on her world-transforming mission by being the church. When the church inhabits the symbolic world of the Bible through the liturgy, and communes together at the Lord's table, she becomes a source of light and life to the world.

Theopolis teaches, develops tools, and fosters networks to assist church leaders throughout the world to form thoroughly biblical, liturgical, and catholic churches. The Theopolis Institute is not a church, but is like scaffolding to assist the church in rebuilding God's heavenly city so that it can effectively carry out her mission of transforming the cities of man.

The Theopolis Institute was established in 2013, but its leaders have been working together to formulate and teach a Theopolitan vision of Bible, liturgy, church, and culture for several decades through James B. Jordan's Biblical Horizons.

The Theopolis Fundamentals Series introduces the Biblical Horizons / Theopolis outlook and agenda to a new generation. The early volumes of the series summarize our convictions about biblical interpretation, liturgical theology and practice, and the church's cultural and political mission. The Fundamentals will be followed by a collection of Theopolis Explorations volumes that will examine Scripture, liturgy, and culture in more depth and detail.

For more information about Theopolis, visit our web site at TheopolisInstitute.com.

THEOPOLITAN LITURGY

PETER J. LEITHART
PHD, UNIVERSITY OF CAMBRIDGE
PRESIDENT OF THEOPOLIS INSTITUTE

BOOKS
AN IMPRINT OF ATHANASIUS PRESS

Theopolitan Liturgy
by Peter J. Leithart

Theopolis Books

Copyright © 2019 Theopolis Books
An Imprint of Athanasius Press

Athanasius Press
715 Cypress Street
West Monroe, Louisiana 71291
www.athanasiuspress.org

Cover design: Ryan Harrison
Typesetting: Christopher D. Kou

ISBN: 978-1-7335356-5-6

All rights reserved. No part of this publication may be reproduced, stored in a retrieval system, or transmitted in any form or by any means—electronic, mechanical, photocopy, recording, or any other—except for brief quotations in printed reviews, without the prior permission of the publisher.

Throughout this book, the author has frequently referred to passages from the New American Standard Bible (NASB) published by the Lockman Foundation. Since the NASB passages quoted represent a minimal part of the original document, it constitutes fair use. All other Bible passages were translated by Peter J. Leithart and are reproduced without any further alterations from Hebrew and Greek texts, which are in the public domain.

CONTENTS

Acknowledgements	vii
Blessed City	ix
To the Reader	xi
Chapter 1 Place	001
Chapter 2 Dialog	024
Chapter 3 Sacrifice	051
Chapter 4 Time	079
Chapter 5 Joy	100
Epilogue	118
For Further Reading	123

ACKNOWLEDGEMENTS

A number of friends and colleagues contributed to the production of *Theopolitan Liturgy*. I am grateful to John Crawford, Jeff Meyers, Jim Jordan, and Alastair Roberts for reading the manuscript and offering their comments. Brian and Ashton Moats proofread the book and saved me from many errors of spelling and grammar. Thanks to Chris Kou for typesetting the book, to John Barach for proof-reading the typeset version, and to Jarrod Richey of Athanasius Press for overseeing the publication process.

This book is dedicated to our forthcoming granddaughter, currently known as "Baby J.J." She's the twelfth of our grandchildren and so holds a typologically significant place in our spreading family tree. As she is born into our family and reborn by water and Spirit into her Father's family, I pray that she will remain always in the company of worshipers in the temple-city, founded on the twelve apostles, whose twelve gates welcome the kings and their treasures.

BLESSED CITY

1. Blessed city, heavenly Salem,
vision dear of peace and love,
who of living stones art builded
in the height of heaven above,
and with angel hosts encircled,
as a bride dost earthward move!

2. From celestial realms descending,
bridal glory round thee shed,
meet for him whose love espoused thee,
to thy Lord shalt thou be led;
all thy streets and all thy bulwarks
of pure gold are fashioned.

3. Bright thy gates of pearl are shining,
they are open evermore;
and by virtue of his merits
thither faithful souls do soar,
who for Christ's dear name in this world
pain and tribulation bore.

4   Many a blow and biting sculpture
     polished well those stones elect,
     in their places now compacted
     by the heavenly Architect,
     who therewith hath willed for ever
     that his palace should be decked.

5   To this temple, where we call thee,
     come, O Lord of Hosts, to-day;
     with thy wonted loving-kindness
     hear thy servants as they pray,
     and thy fullest benediction
     shed within its walls alway.

6   Here vouchsafe to all thy servants
     what they ask of thee to gain,
     what they gain from thee for ever
     with the blessed to retain,
     and hereafter in thy glory
     evermore with thee to reign.

7   Laud and honour to the Father,
     laud and honour to the Son,
     laud and honour to the Spirit,
     ever Three, and ever One,
     consubstantial, co-eternal,
     while unending ages run.

JOHN MASON NEALE

TO THE READER

I should warn you: This is an unusual book on liturgy. It doesn't do some of the things you might expect it to do.

It isn't designed to answer "Should we or shouldn't we?" questions: Should we use leavened or unleavened bread? Should we serve wine in little plastic cups, or use glass, or drink from a common cup? Should the pastor wear a white or a black robe or no robe at all? Should we baptize and commune babies or not? Should we dunk, pour, or sprinkle? Should we use an organ or a band? Should we sing old hymns or praise songs? I have views on all those questions, and I'll occasionally express and defend my views along the way. As every pastor knows, those questions need to be answered. But *Theopolitan Liturgy* isn't written to answer them. It's not a how-to manual.

It's not a book about liturgical *history* either. It's important to know how the church has worshiped through the centuries. Much of the liturgical scholarship of the past century has focused on the history of worship. But that can miss the main point. History isn't the *most* important thing to know. I'm a Bible-thumper at heart, so I believe it's far more important to know what the *Bible* says about liturgy. That's what this book is about.

Every Protestant agrees the Bible is critical. In practice, though, many Christians cobble a liturgical theology and practice from slivers of Scripture—the Gospel accounts of baptism and the Last Supper, a few chapters of 1 Corinthians, scattered snippets from other epistles, and perhaps Revelation. These fragments are barely enough to answer the "Should we or shouldn't we?" questions. They aren't close to sufficient if we're trying to develop a rich biblical theology of worship.

Theopolitan Liturgy works with a larger and more varied pallet. I dip my brush into Genesis, Exodus, Leviticus, Chronicles and Kings, Psalms and the Song of Songs, as well as the Gospels, Pauline Epistles, and the Apocalypse. *Theopolitan Liturgy* provides a thicker, more complex biblical framework for thinking about the liturgy as a whole and for answering the "Should we or shouldn't we?" questions that need to be answered.

My approach leaves many questions open. It may frustrate readers who are looking for quick answers. That can't be helped. The liturgy needs to be shaped by the Word of God, but we can't do that well unless we know what the Word of God actually says about liturgy.

Creation, Culture, Liturgy

I *can* make things a bit easier. I can give away the gist of that framework up front. I'm going to break a basic rule of comedy: I'm going to start with the punch line. I'm going to tell you exactly what this book is about before you read it. If you're the kind of person who skips prefaces, you'll be at a disadvantage. Come to think of it, if you're reading this, you aren't the kind of person who skips prefaces.

Here's the theme: *Theopolitan Liturgy* explores the analogies among and the intertwinings of three levels of reality:

TO THE READER

1) Creation.
2) Culture.
3) Liturgy.

Each chapter explores some feature of created reality, expounds how human culture moves in the grooves of this created reality or distorts this reality, and then explains how Christian liturgy corrects, redirects, glorifies, and completes these features of created and cultural reality.

To see how this works, you've got to understand what I mean by "liturgical." Creation and culture aren't material realities that need to be spiritualized. Creation and culture aren't a secular cake awaiting a liturgical icing.

Creation and culture are *always already* liturgical. Creation emerges from a divine liturgy and lives, moves, and has its being as liturgy. Culture is liturgical all the way down. Liturgy is baked into the cake, not just for Christians, but for everyone: Liturgy crystallizes culture, and culture is the flowering of liturgy. Think Madonna, with a twist: We're liturgical girls and boys living in a liturgical world.

After the fall, we don't stop being liturgical. We become *idolatrously* liturgical. We enact perverse liturgies. That puts us at odds with the design of creation and, worse, with the Creator. It misshapes our cultural worlds.

Jesus dies and rises to restore and glorify creation and culture. His Spirit condemns the perverse liturgies of culture and puts them right. Through the Christian liturgy, the Spirit restores us to *proper* liturgical forms. The liturgy *is* creation and culture being put back in right order.

That's it. That's the punch line. I suspect it's obscure. Let me elaborate.

Theopolitan Vision

The Theopolis Institute tag line is: "Bible. Liturgy. Culture."

The punctuation is misleading. The list isn't over when we get to Bible; it's not "Bible, *period*" or, for you Brits, "Bible, *full stop*." Bible and Liturgy aren't finished without the "Culture" bit. The whole point of the tagline is that these three are inseparably united.

Without the Bible, the church wouldn't know what do to in her liturgy. In fact, there would be no liturgy at all, since the Word read and preached is essential to Christian worship. Instead of a period, we might have written this: Bible→Liturgy. The Bible makes the liturgy.

But it works the other way too. Bibles might exist even if no churches gathered for worship. But the Bible can't do all God wants it to do unless it's read, proclaimed, and taught in the liturgy.

The Bible is God's Word to God's people. As I explained in the first volume of this series, *The Theopolitan Vision*, the church isn't an invisible entity. It's a real-world communion of men, women, and children. That visible communion is the family of the Father, the body of the incarnate Son, the temple of the Spirit.

Gathering and dispersal is the systole and diastole of the church's life. She's the people of the Triune God whether she's gathered for worship or dispersed into the world. But it's in the liturgy that she is publicly, visibly what she in fact is: the family of the Father, the body of the incarnate Son, the temple of the Spirit.

The Bible convicts, commands, encourages, and teaches each of us individually. It does all that when we read silently in privacy. But God gave the Bible to His *church* to build the living temple of saints. God's Word comes from God through His ordained leaders for the church. It's God's community-constructing speech. It's the Bridegroom's love letter to His Bride.

TO THE READER

If we only read the Bible silently in private, God would never speak His Word to His people. Studied in private, the Bible doesn't do its temple-building work. The Bible can't be all it's supposed to be outside the liturgy. God wants to speak to His people, *gathered* as His people.

Plus, the Bible isn't merely spoken *to* us. It's given to be spoken *by* us. The Bible is fulfilled when it's turned into prayer, praise, song, dialogue. That happens in the liturgy.

So we can't separate "Bible" from "Liturgy." Yes, Christian liturgy must be biblical. If it's not biblical, it's worse than useless. God hates it. But we also have to say the Bible is a liturgical book that becomes fully operative in the liturgy. So the relation is really "Bible ←→ Liturgy."

And we can't leave "Culture" dangling out there at the end of the tagline. At Theopolis, we believe churches transform culture when they're shaped by biblical liturgies and liturgical biblicism. Living water flows from the living temple to renew everything from the land to the sea of Gentiles (Ezek 47).

But it works the other way too. Inevitably, culture comes *into* the liturgy.

What do I mean? In this book, I'm using "culture" in a broad sense. It doesn't mean "high culture" or art. It refers to beliefs, habits, customs, rituals, things, norms—a people's entire way of life.

Cultures assume, enforce, and teach norms. They prescribe how we should behave, how we use our bodies meaningfully. *Do* stand to show respect. *Don't* burp at the dinner table. Thou shalt not kill, commit adultery, steal, bear false witness.

Cultures are patterned environments of material things. A group organizes its space. It puts up walls to keep out invaders. It plans cities, builds roads, develops architectural styles. It establishes legal barriers to prevent baddies from prospering. It produces artifacts, tables and chairs, teacups and wine glasses, computers and conference tables, machines with their assembly lines. It produces consumable goods, food and drink and clothing and, in some cases, thousands of varieties of sporty footwear.

Cultures coordinate time. They set aside special occasions, holidays when the norms of the culture are celebrated, when the heroes are remembered. They give shape to work and rest.

Perhaps most obviously, cultures are linguistic. If you're an English speaker, you know you're deep in a foreign country when you can't read any of the road signs and no one can give directions in English.

All these cultural habits and institutions pre-date the arrival of the gospel and the church. Cultures have languages before the missionary comes to town, though missionaries have often created written forms of an existing language. Cultures organize their space and time. They have artistic and musical styles.

All this exists before and outside the liturgy, and it comes into the liturgy, in one way or another. The church uses an existing language, gathers in whatever space the culture provides, adjusts to the time-keeping of the culture.

This looks like a problem. If a pre-existing culture infiltrates the liturgical heart of the church, how can the church *transform* culture? If the city of God is always partly city of man, how can it be an *alternative* to the city of man?

It seems best to raise the barricades and exclude cultural contaminants from the sanctuary. Do the liturgy in Latin since nobody outside the Vatican and classical schools speaks it. Use the same musical, artistic, and architecture styles wherever the churches go. That's the safest option, it seems, because it ensures the liturgy will transcend the particularities of culture.

I'm poking at Roman Catholics in that last paragraph, but we see similar impulses in some branches of Protestantism. Protestants sometimes reduce the cultural contribution to a bare minimum: Use the language of the surrounding culture, but strip all art from the church walls and windows and keep out all the musical instruments. That way, the liturgy won't be cultural. It will be *purely* liturgical.

There's a *potential* problem here. The church is always at risk of becoming a mirror image of the earthly city instead of an outpost of the heavenly city. She must resist conforming to this age. We live toward and according to the standards of the age to come. Some cultural customs, habits, and artifacts must be expelled from the church's worship.

At bottom, though, the "infiltration" of culture into the liturgy isn't surprising or problematic. In fact, it's key to understanding not only the relation of liturgy and culture but to understanding the liturgy itself.

Liturgy and culture don't occupy different worlds. Rather, each inhabits the other: Culture finds a place in the liturgy, and the liturgy inserts itself into culture. It's what theologians call a "perichoretic" relationship. So we can alter the tag line again: Bible ←→Liturgy ←→Culture.

Liturgy shouldn't put up impenetrable barriers to culture. That's sure to make the liturgy culturally irrelevant. Rather, liturgy is culturally transformative only *because* it's permeable to culture.

Liturgy As Christianized Culture

How does this work? Think about language, which I'll talk about at more length in chapter 2. The church uses the culture's pre-existing language in her liturgy. But she says new things. She uses the existing language to call on the Father through the Son in the Spirit. She uses the existing language to announce, "Jesus is Lord." She uses the existing language to say, "Love your enemies."

An existing language enters the liturgy, but the liturgy doesn't leave the language intact. By putting the language to Christian uses, the church refreshes and restores language. She fulfills the original purpose of the language, which is to be a medium of communion between God and human beings, and among human beings. Liturgical language is language in the process of being redeemed.

If liturgy and culture inhabited different worlds, we'd need to build something to bridge the gap. We'd be tempted to alter the liturgy to make it relevant to the culture. If culture already inhabits the liturgy, things look quite different. As we'll see throughout this book, every fundamental component of culture is always already inherent in the liturgy.

The Eucharist serves as a paradigm case. Bread and wine are cultural products, grain and grapes transformed by human labor, technology, and ingenuity. They existed before they became elements of the church's liturgical feast. The liturgy takes up these cultural products and puts them to a new use. In the liturgy, these common foods become means of communion with the Father in the Son by the Spirit. Through the liturgy, the Eucharistic assembly becomes a preview of new Jerusalem, the city from heaven.

In the Eucharistic liturgy, all of *creation* is summoned into the presence of God. In the liturgy, all of *culture* is summoned into the presence of God. In the liturgy, the created and human worlds are brought back into right relation with God.

We can apply that Eucharistic logic to all the other features of culture, which are taken up as features of liturgy. The time of the liturgy is *God's* designated time, the Lord's day. The place is, ideally, a church building, designed and decorated to focus our hearts, minds, and bodies on the work of worship. Our bodily actions aren't just meaningful, but meaningful to God. In most Christian churches throughout history, ministers have worn liturgical clothing to mark their office, a liturgical transfiguration of culture.

TO THE READER

The words we hear are words of God, either directly from the Bible or a pastor's words based on the Bible. We speak and sing words from Scripture or words inspired by Scripture. Thus is language redeemed by its insertion into the liturgy. Liturgical music expresses our joys and laments. It shapes our moods. What's happening in the liturgy is something deeper: Music—a product of cultural transformation of creation—is tuned toward God. Music is fulfilled as a sacrifice of praise.

The liturgy doesn't leave culture behind, not for an instant. Everything in the liturgy is cultural; every cultural element is transformed liturgically. Everything we are and produce—space, time, speech, action, clothing, music, art—is directed toward its ultimate end, our entry into the glory and joy of God.

This is why the liturgy is culturally transformative. It's not that we commune with God and *then* head out to start transforming the world. The world is transformed *in* the liturgy. We keep liturgical time, which changes our time-keeping. We hear and speak Bible, and *right there in the liturgy* we talk differently. We break bread and drink wine, and *right there in the liturgy* agricultural and cultural products are put to new uses.

This world—this real-life cultural world—is the matter of the liturgy, which the liturgy transforms into an effective sign of the coming city of God. The liturgy *is* culture transformed, culture being Christianized. Creation and culture are taken up to become *liturgical* culture.

The chapters that follow examine some of the coordinates of Christian liturgy, which are also the coordinates of human life as such—place, dialogue, sacrifice, time, and joy. Each chapter shows that creation itself is liturgical. Space is created as a temple, language exists for dialogue with God and one another, life is a sacrificial movement of death and resurrection, time is choreographed for liturgical dance, and the world exists to give us a share in the joy of the Father.

Cultures inescapably manifest these created patterns. All cultures organize time and space, use language, offer sacrifice, encourage hope for some form of final bliss. Since Adam, cultures distort these created patterns. We tell lies, brutalize one another in sacrificial slaughter, organize time and space unjustly, hold out hope for false joys. Cultures are idolatrous, perverse variations on the liturgy of creation.

If it is biblically formed, the liturgy enacts the truth about the world. It concentrates creation and culture—space and time, language and sacrifice, joy and feasting—in order to usher creation and culture toward its ultimate fulfillment in the city of God, the heavenly Jerusalem.

Here's the punch line of this little book: The Liturgy is *itself* the first transformation of culture. The Liturgy *is* culture transformed into kingdom.

1   PLACE

Lord, You have been our dwelling place in all generations.
        Psalm 90:1

Some Christians are put off by the word "liturgy." It conjures up images of dank churches full of dull people bumbling and mumbling their way through inexplicable rituals. A liturgical church is, by definition, a dead church, murdered by vain repetitions. If we're merciful, we'll give it a dignified burial.

Liturgy means irrelevance. Only a hidebound traditionalist likes liturgical forms. Liturgical churches pathetically preserve a past that was pretty lame to begin with.

If you want energy and life, you need to find a church with a praise band and a light show. That's where you can *worship*.

So it seems to many Christians.

If that's what you're thinking, I know where you're coming from. I grew up in a liturgical church. The worship was dull and slow. We mumbled our way through. We had no idea why we were doing what we were doing.

I loved parts of it, but I fled at my first opportunity. At twenty, with the brash omniscience of youth, I renounced liturgy with all its pomp and show.

Over the following years, with the help of friends and collaborators, I turned back to liturgy. I'm a convert, or a re-convert. I now believe the church should have a repetitive order of worship, done pretty much the same every week, with pre-written prayers and dialogue, weekly communion, candles, pastors in white liturgical robes. I now believe, in short, the church should worship with an old-fashioned liturgy.

My reasons for re-converting were partly historical. I learned the church's worship has been liturgical until the day before yesterday. The early church developed liturgical forms rooted in the temple and synagogue liturgies of Judaism. The Eastern and Western church pursued distinct trajectories, but both used set forms of prayer and worship. Nearly every Reformer wrote at least one liturgy. Prayer books aren't Catholic. They were introduced at the Reformation.

"Non-liturgical" Christian worship developed in the centuries after the Reformation. They're an aberration. And "non-liturgical" is a ruse anyway. As historian Lori Branch points out, "non-liturgical" churches develop rituals, though they don't always notice. Their rituals are, paradoxically, "rituals of spontaneity."

Even if a church doesn't use a prayer book or print a bulletin, its services fall into repeated patterns. It's pretty much the same thing every week. That's not a criticism. It's good to have liturgical habits. It's the way God wants us to worship. It's the way we're made.

The historical case for liturgy is convincing, but history isn't the most important factor in my re-conversion to liturgy. The *Bible* is. History isn't our ultimate standard for worship or anything else. The *Bible* is.

After all, not everything the church has done in worship is good. Orthodox Christians venerate icons, which the Second Word forbids (Exod 20:4-6). The medieval church largely excluded lay people from the liturgy.

Protestant worship is, I believe, closer to Scripture, but it isn't perfect either. Some Protestant churches wrongly strip art from the place of worship, and some wrongly believe musical instruments are prohibited. Many Anglicans kneel to receive communion, an odd posture if you're eating a celebratory meal. Besides, Protestants differ on all sorts of liturgical issues. Five hundred years after the Reformation, we still can't agree on what happens in holy communion or whether or not to baptize infants.

Unless we have a standard *beyond* history, we can't sort through the good, the bad, and the ugly of the church's liturgical history. Scripture is that standard. It tells us how we're to worship, warns us about false forms of worship, and infuses everything in the liturgy.

I think Christian worship should look a lot like a traditional Lutheran, Anglican, Methodist, or Reformed service. But I don't think those are best because they're Lutheran, Anglican, Methodist, or Reformed. I think they're best because they're *biblical*.

In this book, I'll try to make a *biblical* case for a form of worship that looks a lot like those liturgical services many find so boring. I'll try to get you excited about liturgy by unveiling a little of the Bible's stunning theology of worship.

Let's get something straight at the beginning: Liturgy isn't a marginal issue in Scripture. It's *the* issue. God created the world as liturgical space, and He intends to fill it with joyous, eternal worship. Liturgy is the Alpha and Omega of the biblical story. It's the reason God created human beings and everything else.

To talk about liturgy, we have to talk about everything. Liturgy stretches from creation to the eschaton and to the ages of ages. Amen.

Cosmic Temple

During the first half of the creation week, God forms a "three-story" house—heaven as the roof above, earth as the main floor, the sea as the flooded basement. He spends the second half of the week filling the spaces—with plants, heavenly lights, fish and birds, land animals, and man and woman. After six days of labor, the Lord takes His rest, enthroned on the circle of heaven, delighting in His work.

By the end of the week, God has built a temple. A temple is a dwelling place for a god, and God created the world as His house. Creation is a sanctuary for God's image.

Why think that the cosmic house is a *temple*? Genesis 1 never says that. Are we reading into it? The reason becomes clear when we look at other "creation stories" in the Bible.

Yahweh's instructions concerning the tabernacle are a creation story. They're laid out in seven sections (Exod 25–31), each beginning with the phrase "and Yahweh spoke to Moses." The speeches mimic the creation week. Yahweh speaks *seven* times, and the seventh speech is a Sabbath command (Exod 31:12–17).

The construction of the tabernacle also mimics God's work in creation. First Moses sets up walls, curtains, and covering, *forming* the tabernacle (Exod 40:17–19). Then he places all the furniture, *filling* the tent with the altars, the table, the lampstand, and the ark (Exod 40:20–33).

At the climax, Moses ordains Aaron and his sons as priests, new Adams in the new creation of the tabernacle (Lev 8–9). With His house built, His furniture in place, His servants installed, Yahweh takes His throne above the cherubim in the Most Holy Place. He enters Sabbath (Exod 40:34–38; Lev 9:23–24).

Here's what we learn from Exodus: The design of the tabernacle is described in seven speeches. Its construction mimics the form-and-fill action of God's creative work. The tabernacle is a sanctuary, a dwelling place for God.

From here we can reason backwards: If the tabernacle is a new creation, then creation is the original tabernacle. If the sanctuary is like creation, then creation is a sanctuary.

Creation is an ordered world. The Bible shows it's a particular kind of order, a *temple* order. Creation is a cosmic temple.

As a temple, the universe is a stage for a cosmic liturgy. All the furnishings of creation are directed toward worship. God speaks light into existence to order day and night. On Day 4, He places lights in heaven to mark seasons and appointed times (Gen 1:14). With its rhythm of evening and morning, new moons and solar year, heaven is a liturgical clock, ticking out times of worship.

God fills His temple with liturgical materials and utensils. He creates a watery world, calls plants from the ground, forms animals from the earth. Every one of these things is destined for inclusion in worship. As soon as they're spoken into existence by the mouth of God, created things are vessels of God's house, choreographed into a liturgical dance.

The first liturgy is the liturgy of the world.

Image, Priest, Temple-Builder

Here we have to make things a little more complex. God doesn't create a steady-state world that remains the same from beginning to end. God creates a world of change and movement. He creates a world that will undergo a *history*.

The initial temple isn't supposed to stay just as it is. It's going to change. It's supposed to get better. It's eventually going to be a glorified city-temple. And human beings are the ones who make it better. The cosmic temple is the platform for a cosmic liturgy. The cosmic temple also provides the materials and time for the development of human culture. Culture is the bridge from the first to the final temple.

Ancient temples are homes for a god or a pantheon. At the climax of a temple-building project, the architect-king sets a god's image on its pedestal in the inner sanctuary. Ancient peoples know the god is present because his image is present.

The living God sets the pattern. He does it first. He builds and furnishes a house. At the climax, He sets His image at the center: Man, male and female, in the image and likeness of God (Gen 1:26–28).

Adam and Eve are signs of the Creator's presence in His cosmic temple. By placing them in His world, the Creator claims the universe as His own. Setting His images in His house, He pledges to share His temple with them.

The images of the Creator are, of course, drastically different from the images of false gods. As Psalm 115 says, idols are blind, deaf, and immobile, incapable of smell or speech. Those who worship dead gods die. Idols aren't just dead. They're deadly.

Like the God they image, Adam and Eve have eyes to see, ears to hear, noses to smell, hands to grasp, feet to walk. Adam is a *living* being, the living image of the living God.

This is the foundation for the Second Word Yahweh speaks at Mount Sinai (Exod 20:4–6). He forbids Israel to make images to venerate and serve because the Israelites are *themselves* images. The only images of Yahweh in Israel's sanctuaries are human images: the Aaronic priests and the gathered people.

As living images of the Creator, Adam and Eve are caretakers of the cosmic temple. Creation is a temple, and everything in it is designed as a liturgical vessel. But the world is fulfilled in liturgy only through *us*, priests of the cosmic liturgy. Through men and women, all creation is directed toward worship as we direct creation and all our work in creation toward the end of praise. Created things come to fulfillment as they nestle into the liturgy.

Sometimes created things come *directly* into the liturgy. We baptize with water, plain ol' H_2O. Most often, creation enters the liturgy only after it has been changed, glorified by labor. We turn creation into culture, and we present creation and culture to God in liturgical fulfillment.

This is clear at the end of the Bible, John's vision of new Jerusalem. The city is a glorified garden (Rev 22:1–5). It's also a sanctuary, a cubic Most Holy Place expanded into civic space (Rev 21:1-8). In Revelation, creation is fulfilled as new creation, a completed, glorified cosmic temple. Scripture begins with an initial cosmic temple. It ends with a vision of the final cosmic temple, finalized by our cultural contribution.

The final cosmos is filled with praise. As Revelation 5 opens, John sees a book at the right hand of the One Enthroned. No one can open it, and John laments. If the book remains unopened, God's purposes will not be completed.

Then the Lamb appears. Jesus ascends to take the book, and His ascension touches off radiating, concentric waves of praise: first the living creatures and angelic elders near the throne, then other angels, then "every created thing which is in heaven and on the earth and under the earth and on the sea" (5:13). That is to say, *everything*.

The world won't end in a climate change apocalypse. The world won't end in world war. The world ends in worship, neither a bang nor a whimper but a shout and song of praise.

From cosmic temple to cosmic temple-city: This is what history is all about. God seeks worshipers. He seeks to unite all things into a universal act of worship, and He *will* find what He seeks. Human culture—the realm of our making and doing—is the bridge between the first and final temple, between creation and new creation. Through us, the world becomes what it's created and destined to be.

I realize this may sound a bit mistily mystical, so let me give some examples.

- Trees glorify God by their sheer existence, but they're fulfilled when human beings transform them into musical instruments to accompany song. Creation→culture→liturgy = Created trees→musical instruments→liturgical instruments.
- Do the very stones worship God? Yes. But they're fulfilled as stones by being incorporated into the liturgy. Israel mines gold to make a cover for the ark of the covenant. They dig up gemstones, polish them, and set them in the breastplate of Aaron. Rocks are hewn from a mountain to become walls of Solomon's temple, or of a Gothic cathedral. Again, creation→culture→liturgy.
- Grain yearns for self-sacrifice, to be cut, ground, baked into bread, eaten. Every young grape dreams of being crushed, fermented, and relished at a feast of wine. All food longs to be incorporated into the covenant feast, where the Bride communes at her Husband's table. Bakers make the dreams of grain come true; vintners fulfill the ambitions of young grapes. Creation→culture→liturgy = plants→food→Eucharist.
- Shepherds and herdsman care for animals, so they're able to enter worship. Not all are chosen, but every newborn lamb longs to be transformed to smoke on Yahweh's altar. Sons of the herd come to fulfillment by giving their blood on the altar for atonement.

This is what *things* are for: to become vessels of the liturgy. This is what *human beings* are for: to glorify the cosmic temple by transforming created things into vessels of praise. This is where *everything* is headed: At the last, all the treasures of the nations will adorn new Jerusalem, the completed cosmic temple (Rev 21:24).

PLACE

Pay attention because this is crucial: The liturgy doesn't spiritualize material things. It doesn't turn a secular world into a sacred one. Creation is liturgically designed. It has a liturgical destiny. It's liturgical all the way down. When we worship, we unveil creation's origin and history's hidden destiny. The liturgy anticipates the way the world ought to be and *will* be.

Pattern on the Mountain

We keep making things more complicated, but we haven't quite captured the complexity of the situation. Let's think a little about a specific feature of culture: the organization of space.

Every culture organizes space in one way or another. We draw boundaries and property lines, build walls for houses and factories, erect fences, plan the streets and neighborhoods that make up our cities.

Cultures don't organize space in the same way. Think of the difference between the Shambles in York and the wide sidewalks of old Greenwich Village; between the winding streets of Rome and the geometric grid work of a Midwestern American city; between the makeshift crush of an African shantytown and the elbow room of an American suburb.

We organize space because we're made in the image of God the Builder. With Wisdom at His right hand (Prov 8:22–31), Yahweh lays the foundations of the earth (Psa 104:5; Isa 51:13), sets up pillars (Psa 75:3), and stretches out the curtain of heaven (Psa 104:2; Isa 40:22).

Made in His image, human beings are builders. We, too, set boundaries, lay foundations, stretch out roofs. Yahweh plants a garden for Adam, but Noah himself plants a vineyard. Yahweh builds a cosmic sanctuary, and later Moses pitches Yahweh's tent and Solomon constructs His temple.

Noah, Moses, and Solomon are new and better Adams because they're builders. But no builder is as great as the Last Adam, who constructs a lasting city, the city whose Builder and Maker is God (Heb 11:10), the church whose gates withstand hell's assaults (Matt 16:18), the bridal city Jerusalem.

Adam is created to glorify God's cosmic house. He's created to organize created space to honor God. But how does he know how to build? How does he know what a glorified cosmic temple looks like? Where are the blueprints?

Genesis 2 tells us: The *garden of Eden* is Adam's model. God provides a 3D model to guide the formation of human space. What the garden is, and what happens in the garden, sets the tone for what happens in the liturgy of the world.

Your Sunday School teacher probably told you Adam and Eve lived in a beautiful garden, full of fruit trees and tame animals. That's almost true, but misleading. When God creates the world, it's marked off into *three* areas, and these three areas have different purposes.

At the center of creation is the garden, on the eastern edge of the larger land of Eden ("east in Eden," Gen 2:8). So there's a garden, and there's a land. Outside Eden, God makes other lands. One of them is named: Havilah, where there is gold (Gen 2:11–12). If you wanted to draw a map, you'd mark three areas: garden, land, and world.

Adam and Eve have different tasks in each zone. The garden is the place of worship. How do I know that? Genesis doesn't say it, but the rest of the Bible implies it. Once again, we can think backwards by looking at the garden-like features of the temple and tabernacle:

- The temple is built on a mountain, Moriah (2 Chr 3:1). Eden, too, is on a mountain (Ezek 28:12–14).
- The tabernacle and temple have golden lampstands molded

to look like trees. At the door of the temple, Solomon sets up two giant bronze pillars with capitals like lily blossoms. The cedar walls of the temple are carved with palm trees. All these are reminiscent of Eden, with its real trees with real fruit and flowers.

- Yahweh promises to meet Israel at the tabernacle and temple, and He meets Adam and Eve in the garden.
- After Adam and Eve are driven from the garden, Yahweh sets cherubim at the gate to keep them out (Gen 3:24). We don't hear about cherubim again until Yahweh tells Moses to put cherubic figures on the ark of the covenant (Exod 25:8–22) and weave them into the tabernacle curtains (Exod 26:1, 31). Why would Yahweh tell Moses to put cherubim in the tabernacle unless it's a new garden?
- Adam is placed in the garden to "serve and guard" (Gen 2:15). In the Old Testament, those verbs describe the work of Levites and priests (Num 1:53; 3:8–10; Deut 10:8). Adam serves as guardian priest of the garden of God.

Of course, the tabernacle and temple are built *after* the fall. That's why only priests can go in, and only partway. Under the Torah, even Israel isn't ready to re-enter the presence of God. Aaron and his sons are new Adams in a new garden, but Israel the new Eve can't draw near. Israel's sanctuaries are garden settings in a post-fall world.

If the garden is a temple, it's a scale model of creation as a whole. God creates a cosmic temple; He plants a garden-temple. He wants the former to become like the latter. The garden previews the destiny of the universe, which will one day resemble Eden (Rev 22:1–5).

God makes other places too. Outside the garden, Adam and Eve don't worship in a direct way. They have a different task. God blesses them to multiply and fill the earth, and to subdue and rule it (Gen 1:28). They don't need to subdue the garden.

It's already subdued. What they need to subdue is the rest of the world. But if the garden doesn't need to be tamed, it does need to be *adorned*.

Here's what's supposed to happen: One day Adam ventures down the river Pishon from Eden to Havilah and sees shiny things on the ground (Gen 2:10–12). "Those are pretty," he thinks. "I'm going to take one home." Then he thinks: "That's glorious, like the glory of the Lord. I'll take some back to the garden and pretty it up a bit."

Adam is subduing and taking dominion over the earth. He discovers new things and uses them to make the glorious world more glorious. He discovers new things to glorify the garden-temple of God.

Adam is a priest in the garden. He's a king in the world, filling and ruling with Eve his queen. His work in the world outside is oriented toward the garden. He works so he can offer the fruit of his labor in worship.

But remember: The creation isn't designed to stay as-is. Even before sin, Adam and Eve are supposed to change things. God tells them, "Be fruitful, multiply, and fill the earth." As human beings spread over the earth, they can't all gather in the garden of Eden for worship. What do they do?

They set up *other* places of worship. A temple goes up in Havilah. Adam and Eve's children follow the Tigris and set up a sanctuary in Assyria. They plant a garden on the Euphrates. Eventually, if everything goes well, there will be places of worship on the shores of what we call the South China Sea, along the banks of the mighty Mississippi, in the jungles of Africa.

What do these sanctuaries look like? Adam's descendants will set up sanctuaries to resemble the garden of Eden, the original pattern on the mountain. As human beings take dominion over the earth, they plant and build new Edens everywhere they go. Two millennia on, the world will be dappled with lush sacred parks in the middle of every city around the world. Ten millennia on, and the world will be well on its way to becoming entirely a garden-city.

The first Eden sets the pattern for other sanctuaries. It also sets the pattern for the *world*. The multiplied gardens aren't supposed to be green oases in a howling brown wilderness. They're supposed to be gardens of worship in an increasingly gardenified world.

There are fruit trees in the sanctuary and orchards and vineyards outside. Adam names animals in the garden, and shepherds tend animals in their fields. Adam meets Eve in the sanctuary, and their children establish homes and families. The garden is an enclosed space, and outside the garden they build houses, towns, and garden-cities. Beautifying a beautiful creation, we fulfill the destiny of the cosmic temple. Through our cultural labor, we form creation as a home for God.

What about the third zone of creation, the *land* of Eden? What's *that* for? It's not like other lands. It's the land where God's garden is, and so it belongs to God in a unique way. It's a kind of holy land in the original creation.

We know the land of Eden is on higher ground than the garden. A spring springs up in Eden and flows through the garden (Gen 2:10) to become four rivers. The garden is somewhere between the highest spot in Eden and other lands.

Eden is the throne-land, where Yahweh rules. Adam and Eve start out in the garden, with Adam as priest leading Eve in serving God. But they're created to become kings. As they subdue the world, they ascend to the high place of Eden to rule alongside the Creator. Like the world, the land is to resemble the garden. Adam and Eve are called to transform the land.

Three zones: garden, land, world. Three assignments: worship in the garden, enthronement and rest in the land, and conquest and rule in the world. This is how the space of the original creation was divvied up.

As Adam and Eve's children spread out from Eden, they carry this map with them. Wherever they go, they're to plant garden-sanctuaries for worship and set up places for rest and rejoicing. Wherever they go, they're to remake the world according to the pattern of the garden. Their cultural labor moves the initial temple of creation toward its fulfillment as new creation.

To sum up, we've got to put two things together here. On the one hand, God gives Adam and Eve the garden as a *model* for the world. Man's purpose is to transform creation into sanctuary or, to say the same thing, to transform creation into God's garden-city. History is the gardenification of creation. Or the "Edenification." Or the New-Jerusalemization. You get the idea.

On the other hand, the garden serves as Adam and Eve's *place of worship*. It's the first liturgical space.

Add these up, and we draw a crucial conclusion about worship and liturgical space: Liturgy and liturgical space model the future creation. What we do in the liturgy is what we hope will one day happen everywhere at all times. Liturgical space serves as the template for transforming the world. Our worship space should anticipate what the world will eventually be. When we enter, we should sigh and think, "Ah, yes. Someday the whole world will look like *this*."

Dis-Placement

Almost immediately, of course, it goes badly wrong. Adam sins in the garden (Gen 3), Cain sins in the field (Gen 4), and the sons of God intermarry with daughters of men in the world (Gen 6). Adam fails in worship; Cain assaults his brother rather than guarding him; the sons of God compromise their witness by allying with the wicked.

Adam is made and placed in the garden (Gen 2:7–8), in the

presence of God. After he sins, he and his wife are cast out to the east, and the way of return is guarded by cherubim with flaming swords (Gen 3:24). Since Adam's sin, man is *dis*placed.

And the displacement continues. After Cain kills Abel, he's cast out of the field, forced further east, further from the face of God, out to the land of Nod (Gen 4:16). When sons of God marry the daughters of men, the world is filled with violence, and God sends a flood to cast out everyone except Noah and his family.

Adam is created to turn the world into a garden, to glorify the cosmic temple. Instead, his sin kicks the first domino that eventually de-creates the world, turning it back to watery emptiness. Instead of a worldwide garden, Adam's descendants leave behind an endless waste. Devastation reigns over the world.

Adam's descendants are builders, but their construction is a form of destruction. Cain builds a city, but it's founded on the blood of his innocent, faithful brother (Gen 4:17). Cain's city is the first of the Bible's many wicked cities, of which Babel is most famous.

The men of Babel refuse to spread over the earth, raise a tower to connect earth to heaven, and build a city in defiance of God (Gen 11:1–9). Babel's tower is a sanctuary, but an idolatrous one. The city aims to unite mankind in rebellion. In Sodom, the town square isn't a place of welcoming hospitality. Instead, strangers are subjected to homosexual assault (Gen 18). While Israel is in Egypt, Pharaoh builds storage cities by beating down the people of God (Exod 1).

Israel is no better. Gibeah is Little Sodom (Judg 19). Late in his reign, Solomon turns idolatrous and Pharaonic, builds shrines to idols, and so provokes an exodus of ten tribes (1 Kgs 11–12). Isaiah calls Jerusalem "Sodom" because Zion, like Sodom, abuses the poor. The bridal city becomes a harlot (Isa 1:10–31). In Isaiah's day, wealthy Israelites add field to field to keep their brothers at a distance (Isa 5:8–10). Jeremiah calls the temple a "den of thieves" (Jer 7), and on his tour of the temple, Ezekiel finds it's as choked with idols as any pagan temple (Ezek 8–11).

Jesus echoes Jeremiah and laments over Jerusalem, the city that kills prophets. He warns the city walls will be dismantled, not one stone on another. What the priests fear comes to pass, as the Romans take away the Jews' "place" (John 11:48). Displaced, man forms spaces of violence, injustice, and oppression. Our cultural efforts don't form a bridge from Eden to new Jerusalem; more often, they form a bridge to hell.

Of course, this isn't ancient history. All over today's world, men and women damage God's cosmic temple. Man still organizes space in insolent disobedience to the Lord of the temple.

We build grand temples to Satanic idols. Today, tens of millions are displaced by war, persecution, or other forms of injustice and violence. We exploit creation until forests are charred deserts. We zone our cities to keep untouchables and undesirables on the far side of the tracks, while those who can afford it live in safe complacency within their gated, well-policed neighborhoods. Our spaces don't express love of God and neighbor, but blasphemy and hatred for strangers.

After Adam's sin, the spatial structure of the original creation is still in place. Human life is still organized around three spaces with their three activities: worship in the garden, rest in the home and throne land, dominion in the world. But in every place, human life is corrupted: Idols occupy gardens; abuse is rampant in homes; war, rivalry, and greed devastate the world. After Adam's sin, men and women are displaced, without true sanctuary. We're strangers in God's cosmic temple, searching for a place to call home.

Garden in the Wilderness

God doesn't leave us without a witness. He gives Adam a model home. After Adam's sin, He keeps giving models to shape our work within His cosmic temple. In a world turned to desert, God gives us gardens of hope. In a world of displacement, *God gives places.*

These places are redeemed spaces, spaces where the world is in the process of being recreated, where the liturgical vessels of creation are being put to their proper, liturgical uses. These sanctuaries are God's answer to Babel and Sodom. Instead of raising a defiant tower toward the sky, these sanctuaries descend from heaven, made according to a heavenly pattern to connect heaven and earth (Exod 25:9, 40; Heb 8:5).

At these places, Yahweh is present in glory. Strangers aren't raped, but welcomed. Slaves, the poor, and the weak share a feast with the free, the rich, and the strong (Deut 12:12, 18; 14:29; 16:11, 14). *Here* is a place for the displaced.

These sanctuaries are products of human labor. They're cultural artifacts, full of cultural artifacts: Altars, tables, lampstands, the ark, bread, beer, wine. But they're products of *Spirit-led* labor (cf. Exod 31:1–11; 35:30–35), and so they're outposts of new creation.

In the sanctuaries, the rebellious organization of space is reversed. Space is put to its proper use as space for worship. In the sanctuary, creation transformed into culture is fulfilled in liturgy. The sanctuaries give a small glimpse of creation's destiny to be fulfilled as God's cosmic temple.

Israel's sanctuaries are sacred places, made holy by the glory of the Lord (Exod 29:43). For Israel, "sacred" means "off-limits." Like the garden, the tabernacle and temple are prohibited places, guarded by cherubim. Only consecrated priests are allowed to enter Yahweh's house. Israel isn't yet holy enough to enter the holy space.

It's important to emphasize again: Liturgical space isn't "spiritual" space in a "secular" world. Liturgical space is *rightly-ordered, rightly-used space* in a displaced world. Liturgical space is where the future city is taking form within the cities of men. Liturgical space is future space present in the present.

In the Old Testament, God's place doesn't stay in place because people keep spoiling it. First, God's place is the garden. Cain and Abel have to bring their offerings to the gate of the garden because they can't get in. Later, Abram sets up altars throughout the land (Gen 12:7; 13:4, 18; 22:9).

After the exodus, Yahweh instructs Israel to pitch His royal tent at the foot of Sinai. In the early days of Samuel, Philistines attack and leave the tent in tatters (1 Sam 4–6). For a century, Israel worships in two places—the tent for the ark, which David eventually takes into Jerusalem (2 Sam 6), and the Mosaic tabernacle, which ends up at Gibeon (1 Kgs 3:3–5).

Solomon puts the pieces back together and builds a permanent house for Yahweh, the temple on Mount Moriah. But Israel abuses that house, so Yahweh sends in Nebuchadnezzar to rip it apart and cart it away in pieces to Babylon. Joshua and Zerubbabel build a new temple, and Ezra and Nehemiah complete the Lord's "house" by extending it to the edges of the city. Jerusalem becomes a "holy city," an urban temple, anticipating the final temple from heaven. But the second temple doesn't last either. Before the apostles die, not one stone is left on another.

So, where's the place of worship? Where's the garden in the wilderness of the world? Eden? Bethel? Sinai or Shiloh? Gibeon or Moriah? It keeps moving. There's no permanent place for worship. That's a problem. If there's no liturgical space, there's no redeemed space. Can displaced humanity find a place if God keeps moving?

Plus, all these places are a long way from almost everyone. Suppose you're an Ethiopian who wants to worship the God of Israel. You can pray from anywhere. But you can't enter fully into worship without making a long trek to Jerusalem. If you're a eunuch in the court of Queen Candace (Acts 8), you can afford the trip. If you're a peasant, you can't.

That distance is a problem. Yahweh is the Creator. He's the source of all good. He's the God of Eden, who offers the fruit of the tree of life. He's the God of Sinai, who speaks words of life. If you want to *live*, you need to get close to Him. But He's a long way away. Even if you get to His house, He might not be there anymore. While you were traveling, He might have moved from His polluted house to Babylon.

But there *is* something constant: *Yahweh*. Wherever and whenever people call upon the name of the Lord, He's there. He's there in Eden, walking among the trees. He appears to Abram and Jacob, and they build altars. He comes down in a fiery cloud on Sinai, and His glory fills the completed tabernacle and later the temple. When Yahweh casts Israel into exile, Yahweh goes into exile with them (Ezek 8–11), sharing the curse He Himself imposes on His people. Can Israel sing Yahweh's song in a strange land (Psa 137)? Sure, because the living temple is with them.

Where is the place of worship? *Yahweh* is the place of worship. He's the garden in the wilderness of the world. Generation after generation sings Psalm 90: "Lord, thou has been our hiding place in all generations" (v. 1).

All the places of worship in the Bible reinforce this truth. They're architectural representations of the glory of Yahweh. It's as if Yahweh's luminous glory cloud precipitated as fabric, wood, gems, gold, silver, bronze—as if the uncreated splendor of God took solid shape in blocks of stone and slabs of wood.

This truth becomes more fully evident in the new covenant. Since Jesus died and rose, there has been no single earthly sanctuary. The *people* are the temple, made of living stones (1 Pet 2:4–8). *We* are God's house, which means *we* are the created glory that manifests the uncreated glory of God. And it means that wherever the people gather, *there* is liturgical space because the Lord God Almighty and the Lamb are our temple (Rev 21:22; cf. John 4:15–26). The living God makes room for us *in Him*.

The liturgy is an entry into *this* place, the place that is God Himself. That tells us something about how the liturgy should run. In many churches, worship begins with an invocation of God's name: "In the Name of the Father, and of the Son, and of the Holy Spirit." That's God's welcoming invitation, a sign He *wants* you to come into His house. It also announces a *destination*. You enter a church building, but that's a portal to the heavenly sanctuary. It's a gate into the true temple, the Father who dwells in the Son. By the Spirit, they dwell in us and we in them.

Worship, in short, has a Triune shape. By that, I don't merely mean Christians worship the Triune God—the Father, Son, and Spirit; the One enthroned, the Lamb, and the seven Spirits who are the eyes of the Lamb. That *is* the God we worship. But we need to think more deeply. Christians don't toss up prayers and praise toward a Triune God who lives at a great distance in heaven. Christian worship is worship *within* the Trinity. Gathering as church, we gather *in* the Triune God.

We are "in Christ," joined to the Son by the Spirit who is poured out on and in us. As the Father is in the Son and the Son in the Father, so they dwell in us by the Spirit (John 17:21). And we dwell in them. We are incorporated into the Triune communion.

That Triune fellowship is an eternal communion of prayer, communion, praise, mutual glorification. The Father glorifies the Son with the glory of the Spirit, and the Son glorifies the Father by the same Spirit. The Father humbles Himself to exalt the Son, and the Son to exalt the Father. The Father praises the Son through the Spirit, and the Son praises the Father in the same Spirit. The God who creates the universe as a cosmic temple is *Himself* an eternal divine temple. God is a dwelling for God. In Christ, He invites us, displaced sons of Adam, to share *His* place.

Our prayers aren't merely ours but are joined to the prayers of the Son as He cries "Abba" to His Father. Our wordless groans are carried by the Spirit, who groans within us in unutterable laments (Rom 8:18–25). When we praise the Father, we join the Son's praise. When we honor the Son, we are caught up by the Spirit in the Father's glorification of the Son.

Christian worship is never—it *cannot* be—a merely human activity. Christian worship is always our incorporation into the eternal liturgy that is the life of the Triune God.

Gardenified Churches

God is our liturgical space. In an ultimate sense, He's all we need. The church can worship in catacombs and caves if she needs to. God will hear and delight in our praises. *He* is redeemed space, the one safe place in a world of displacement.

But the church has never been satisfied with catacombs and caves. She's built buildings for worship. Biblically, that's the right instinct. The liturgy redeems place and therefore should take place in places. So the church has rightly sought to make the reality of God's presence public, visible in the world. Whenever the church has the freedom to build, she has carved out spaces for liturgy. Following Scripture, she tries to reflect God's glory in stone, glass, and wood.

Some Christian traditions describe churches as "sacred space," but that phrase is liable to be misunderstood. As I said above, in Israel "Sacred" is a "No Entry" sign. Israelites can't enter the temple because the temple is holy and they're not.

The Christian church doesn't have *any* sacred spaces in this sense. Jesus opened the way and brought us all in. He tears the veil that separated the sacred space from the outer court. In Him, we're all saints, "holy ones," because we're united to Jesus through baptism. Every believer has access to the heavenly sanctuary; all are "in Christ," at home in the eternal communion of Father, Son, and Spirit. *We* are the glory that consecrates the Lord's house.

Under the new covenant, places are "consecrated" in the way everything else is: by thanksgiving, the Word, and prayer (1 Tim 4:4–5). Every saint consecrates everything he receives with gratitude and prayer. Every congregation makes a church building holy by giving thanks.

But holy things aren't forbidden things and holy spaces are no longer closed spaces. Christian churches shouldn't be designed to exclude or to communicate that the laity is further away than the clergy. Like the bread of the Lord's Supper, a church building is a "holy thing for holy people."

Christian churches have been, and should be, Bible-made-buildings. Like Eden, the tabernacle, and the temple, churches have often been built on an east-west axis, with the congregation facing east, enthroned with Christ and awaiting the sunrise from on high. They should resemble the garden of God. The roof vault looks like the ribs inside a ship because the church is Noah's ark on the dangerous seas of the world. Christian churches have been, and should be, architectural embodiments of God's glory. Cathedral spires soar up toward heaven. Stained glass windows rainbow the sunlight. Statues and pictures of heroes and saints remind us we worship with the dead as well as the living.

Christians who built such churches understood what they were doing. They understood the creation as a temple. They knew culture is the bridge between the initial and the final temple. They put their cultural skills, styles, tools, and materials to use in building churches that anticipate the new heavens and new earth, the heavenly temple-city. They seasoned the world with sanctuary-gardens, outposts of new creation. We should continue their work. If you walk into church and groan, "I hope the new creation is *nothing* like this," something is badly wrong. We aim at a gardenified world. Gardenify the liturgical spaces first.

The Scriptures are written for our edification, Paul says. Israel repeatedly spoils her places of worship. By her idolatry, injustice, sin, and hypocrisy, she pollutes Yahweh's places and He abandons them. He doesn't automatically stay with the church either. We don't trap him in our cathedrals, no matter how glorious they are. If a church persists in sin, Jesus removes the lampstand, which plunges the church into darkness. He will spit us from His mouth (Rev 3:16). Cathedrals can become hollow shells, or worse, synagogues of Satan.

Liturgical space is where the Spirit is redeeming created place, where He's remaking the world's space into a glorified cosmic temple. But He doesn't redeem our places if we defy Him. Liturgical space isn't worth anything if we quench the Spirit. The liturgy won't do its culture transforming work if we grieve the Spirit of the liturgy. It calls us to faith, dogged allegiance to King Jesus.

But: As we keep in step with the Spirit, liturgical space spreads across the planet—space devoted to the worship of God, redeemed space that begins to redirect all space toward its intended purpose, space used the way the whole creation is designed, and destined, to be used. As liturgical places multiply, the world is increasingly gardenified. It increasingly comes to resemble what it will be: new Jerusalem, the garden city that descends from heaven.

2 DIALOG

Then God said, "Let there be light"; and there was light.
            Genesis 1:3

Remember those dank cathedrals with the dull repetitions I mentioned at the beginning of chapter 1? They're not just dank and dull. They're also very, very quiet, hushed even.

Not *completely* quiet, mind you. If you time-traveled with The Doctor back to a medieval French church, you'd hear a *few* things. Priests and monks chanting Psalms. A priest reading Scripture and whispering the *Hoc est* ("This is") at the altar, confecting bread into the body of Christ. If you time-traveled to the right century, you'd hear a sermon, maybe from an itinerant friar.

But you'd notice something about the sound. It's almost all in Latin. That's strange, because the people speak French or some precursor of French. All over Europe, all Catholic churches sound the same. Whether you step into a church in England or Poland or Norway, the priest is speaking Latin.

There's something attractive about that, of course. Today, you can visit two churches in the same town, from the same denomination, and the worship services can be entirely different.

A little uniformity is a good thing.

Mostly, though, it's a bad deal to have a Latin liturgy for people who don't speak Latin. The faithful gather in the presence of the Lord, and He speaks in an unknown tongue. No wonder medieval Christians turned to relics and statues and other objects of devotion. God wasn't talking much.

You'd notice another thing too: The congregation doesn't say much either. They don't know Latin, so they can't chant along with the hymns. They can't understand the Scripture readings and wouldn't recognize the "Hoc est" even if they could hear it.

Some of them learn a few snatches here and there. They learn to recognize some Bible words. If there's a sermon, it's in the vernacular, so they can follow along with that. If they attend Mass often enough, they'll pick up some of the phrases of the altar liturgy. Even so, they don't speak. Worship isn't a dialogue.

There are theologians out there who will tell you hushed reverence is the way Christians participate in the liturgy. They might quote Habakkuk: "The Lord is in His holy temple. Let all the earth keep silent before Him" (Hab 2:20). Silence, they'll say, isn't exclusion. Silence is what makes worship spiritual. Quietness is next to godliness.

There's a place for silence in the Christian life and the liturgy. But the accent of Scripture is entirely in the opposite direction. The God of the Bible *speaks*, and worship is a dialogue between the speaking God and His listening, and speaking, people.

Liturgy of the World

Remember from the last chapter: God created the world as a cosmic temple, Adam as priest, and everything else as a vessel of a cosmic liturgy. History is a cosmic liturgy. The *word* is at the center of the liturgy of the world. History begins with a word from God, and at every moment everything is sustained by the word of the Lord.

Genesis 1 introduces God to us. What do we learn about Him? First we find out He's the Creator of heaven and earth. Then we learn He is or has a Spirit. We're only three verses in when He speaks His first words: "Let there be light." "God speaks" is one of the very first things we learn about Him.

He keeps talking until there's heaven above, earth beneath, waters under the earth. He keeps talking until heaven is filled with lights, the sea teems with fish, birds fly over the face of the sky, and animals, creeping things, and men and women are multiplying on the face of the earth.

He speaks to the earth, and it sprouts grass and trees. He speaks to the fish and birds and animals, and they multiply. The Creator is King, who rules His creation through His word, by issuing decrees.

When God first spoke creation into existence, there was nothing there to respond to Him. He didn't find light lurking in a seedy bar and ask it to come out into the open to dispel the darkness. He said the word "Light" when there was no light, and then there *was* light.

There's no more fundamental reason for the existence of the world than God's Word. There isn't some more basic "essence" or "nature" that determines that the world is and what it is. God's *word* is the foundation.

It's not quite accurate to say things exist to respond to God. More profoundly, we exist *as* response to God's almighty summons. Light doesn't have the power to be light on its own. Without the divine "Let there be," light isn't. It doesn't exist and then respond to God. Its very existence is a dialogic response that is possible only because of the Creator's word. God's first word enables creation to respond.

Now that things exist, things respond to God's word. But they are what they are and continue to be what they are because they are engaged in a dialogue with the Creator.

This is how the world works, even now. Every morning, He commands the sun to repeat yesterday's performance. Every evening, He tells the sun to descend in a burst of glory, so the moon and stars can take their place on the darkened stage of the sky.

His voice splits cedar trees, makes the earth shake, bursts out in flame, makes the deer calve and strips the forest bare (Psa 29). He commands the angels who are His ministering spirits (Psa 91:11–12).

Why is there something rather than nothing? Because in the beginning, God called things into existence. Why do things continue to exist rather than blipping out of being? Because God *keeps* speaking them.

Man is His primary dialogue partner. He creates mankind and immediately starts talking to us. He gives Adam a command and comes back to see if he's obeyed it. He confronts Cain with his sin and warns Cain's brothers not to take vengeance. He tells Noah He's about to flood the earth and gives him a plan for a saving ark.

He talks to Abraham, Hagar, Isaac, and Jacob. He speaks to Moses at the burning bush and to Israel at Sinai. He speaks to Joshua and Gideon and David and Solomon. Prophets speak because the "Word of Yahweh" places words in their mouths.

When He's not talking, He communicates in other ways—through Joseph's dreams and visions, through Solomon's dreams, through Daniel's ecstasies.

He speaks as God. His words manifest His character. His words are true. He speaks with authority (and not as the scribes). His words are powerful. They accomplish what He intends. He speaks to enter into intimate communion with us.

Since God's words are the words of God, we should respond to them as such. When He makes a promise, we should trust it.

When He says something is true, we should believe it. When He commands, we should obey. When He summons us to rejoice in song, we sing.

God speaks in many portions and in many ways. Our lives are surrounded and infused with His words. We are made to answer; we are made *as* an answer to His creative word. We answer in the portions and ways His words demand.

Everything in our lives is shaped by how we answer His words. If we trust His promises, He proves trustworthy. If we believe what He says, we won't be disappointed. If we obey His commands, we walk in the way of life.

We often do the opposite. He promises, but we doubt. He asserts, but we disbelieve. He commands, but we disobey. Doubt, disbelief, and disobedience lead to frustration and death, eventually eternal death.

Every moment of life and our final destiny in life are determined by our response to the Lord in the liturgy of the world. It's determined by how we answer the word of the Lord. It's determined by our performance in the dialogue of life.

That doesn't just apply to individual men and women. It applies to families, nations, and churches too. The future of a nation depends on whether or not it responds rightly to the word of God. Rulers should honor the King, and He shatters the ones who don't (Psa 2). The same goes for churches. In His messages to the churches of Asia (Rev 2-3), Jesus warns He will remove the lampstand from unrepentant churches. The future of a church depends on its responsiveness to God's word.

This is the liturgical movement of history, the liturgy of the world: God speaks, human beings and communities respond faithfully or not, and their future is determined by that response.

That destiny is the result of a further word from God. He *initiates* the liturgy of history by speaking. He *ends* the liturgy of history with a word of final judgment. History—and every segment of history—is suspended between God's first and final word.

We can see this pattern in the creation week. God speaks light into existence and speaks again to call it good. He speaks to divide waters above from waters below, and water from land, and then speaks again to pronounce it good. He speaks plants and heavenly lights, fish and birds and land animals, then speaks His approval of what He has made.

Each of us and all peoples are suspended between word and word. God speaks, humans and nations answer, and He speaks a second word of evaluation and judgment.

He commands Adam (Gen 2) and then curses after Adam disobeys (Gen 3). He tells righteous Noah to build an ark, and, when Noah obeys, He saves him from the flood (Gen 8–10). When Abram believes His promises, He judges Abram as righteous (Gen 15). He enters into covenant with Israel, promising to bless their obedience and threatening to curse their unfaithfulness with exile (Lev 26; Deut 28). He instructs kings (Deut 17) and takes ten tribes when Solomon violates every royal command (1 Kgs 11–12).

He commands Pharaoh to let Israel go, and when he refuses, He sends plagues and Passover. He summons Assyrians and Babylonians to discipline Israel, but when they overstep their mandate, He punishes them for their pride (Isa 10).

Nations and individuals don't succeed or collapse by accident. God doesn't speak a first word then leave things to take their "natural" course. History is surrounded and embraced by His speech. He speaks the first *and* the last word. The word of the Lord is the Alpha *and* the Omega of creation's and humanity's history.

Creation exists by the power of the word. Creation moves and changes by the power of the word. Everything that is exists as a dialogic being, as a response to God's speech.

The liturgy of the church takes place within this cosmic liturgy of the world. The church's liturgy isn't a retreat from this world. The church's liturgy concentrates the liturgy of history. In the church's liturgy, we carry on a properly ordered dialogue within the dialogue of creation and history.

Liturgy of the Word

The God of the Bible is a communicative God, and not just in relation to the creation. He's an *eternally* communicative God. John draws back the veil to reveal this at the beginning of his Gospel. God the Creator has a Word who is "toward" Him, a Word who *is* God. *This* Word created the world (John 1:1–5).

God doesn't start conversing when He makes creatures to converse with. He *is* an eternal conversation. From forever to forever, the Father has spoken His Word by the breath of His Spirit. The Father cannot speak His Word without hearing the Word speak back. So, from forever to forever, by the same Spirit, the Word responds to the Speaker.

God doesn't *happen* to speak. He doesn't happen to converse. He *is* Word. His life, the Triune life, is an eternal trialogue.

Now, if you go to visit *this* God in His house and He doesn't say anything, you know you're being left out. You *know* there's a conversation going on because there's *always* a conversation going on, and you're not part of it.

Think of it this way: Your best friend invites you to dinner, but his family spends the evening speaking Obenglobish. Unless you're in on the joke, you'll feel frustrated, confused, left out. You'll suspect your friend is playing an elaborate trick.

God *hasn't* played an elaborate trick. He doesn't invite us to His house and sit in sullen, stern, or sanctified silence throughout our visit. He invites us *so that* He can speak to us.

It's even better than that. The conversable God doesn't speak from a great distance. He doesn't speak from behind a veil. He's removed the veil and invites us in. He ushers us into the new sanctuary, heaven itself. He gives us access to the ultimate temple, which is "God and the Lamb" (Rev 21:22).

Let me say it more forcefully: In worship, *we're brought into the Triune conversation*. We're *in* the Word, the incarnate Son, Jesus the anointed King. In and with Jesus, we speak to the Father by the Spirit. Through Jesus and His Spirit-breath, the Father speaks to us. Our words to God and His to us are folded into the eternal trialogue of the eternally conversable Triune God.

It's no accident that throughout the Bible, worship is a response to God's word, a dialogue between the Lord and His people:

- As we saw in chapter 1, the Garden of Eden is the original micro-cosmic sanctuary, the place where Yahweh commands Adam and then returns to evaluate Him, to bless or to curse.
- When the flood subsides, Yahweh commands Noah to come out of the ark, along with his family and all the animals. Noah answers by building an ark altar and offering ascension offerings from every clean animal. When Yahweh smells the soothing aroma, He promises never again to curse the land and to maintain the regular cycles of the seasons (Gen 8:13–22). The sequence is: Yahweh commands→Noah obeys and makes offerings→Yahweh promises.
- When Abram first enters the land on his journey from Ur, Yahweh meets him at Shechem and promises to give the land to his descendants. Abram responds by building an altar. Abram camps between Bethel and Ai, builds an altar, and calls on the name of Yahweh (Gen 12:4–9). The sequence is: Yahweh commands and promises→Abram obeys and builds altars and calls on Yahweh. Abram's worship is a dialogue with the God who promises.
- Moses is the first man to stand on "holy ground" (Exod 3:5) when Yahweh appears to Him at the burning bush. The entire scene is a conversation between the Lord and Moses, at the place where Yahweh will later cut covenant with Israel.

- Sinai is a covenant-cutting event. Following the Lord's instructions, Israel assembles at the foot of the mountain to offer ascension offerings and sacrifices. Yahweh thunders out the Ten Words, then reveals His commandments and statutes to Moses. When Moses brings the word from the mountain, Israel shouts, "All the words Yahweh has spoken, we will do" (Exod 19:1—24:3).
- David writes Psalms and assigns others to write Psalms (e.g., Asaph). Most of the Psalms are written in two-line verses designed to be sung antiphonally, that is, in dialogue:

"Yahweh, how my adversaries have increased!
Many are rising up against me" (Psa 3:1).

"The voice of Yahweh shakes the wilderness;
Yahweh shakes the wilderness of Kadesh" (Psa 29:8).

"Whoever secretly slanders his neighbor, him will I destroy;
No one who has a haughty look and an arrogant heart will I endure" (Psa 101:5).

- After Solomon finishes the temple, he dedicates it with a series of offerings. But the heart of the temple dedication is a long prayer (1 Kgs 8; 2 Chr 6) about future prayer. Solomon asks Yahweh to respond to prayers directed toward the house. Whatever Israel suffers—famine, drought, defeat, invasion, exile—Solomon asks Yahweh to hear them when they turn to the house for healing. He even asks Yahweh to answer Gentiles who trust Him. In response, Yahweh promises to place His eyes, ears, and heart in the house. He will hear and see, and He will answer. Solomon's temple is a house of prayer for the nations, where distressed people can seek relief in response to Yahweh's promises. It's a place of healing conversation with the conversable God.

- Once Israel settles in the land, most of Israel's liturgical life doesn't take place at the tabernacle or the temple. Men are required to travel to the central sanctuary three times a year, for Passover, Pentecost, and the Feast of Booths. They don't go to the sanctuary every week. Holy convocations happen every Sabbath (Lev 23:3), but they happen in local assemblies scattered throughout the land. No animal offerings are permitted at these "synagogues." Priests and Levites, who live in towns throughout Israel, teach Torah, lead prayers, and lead singing. By the time of Jesus, we know what the synagogue liturgy looks like. It's a dialogue, just like every form of worship in the Bible.

Love Song

Leviticus looks like an exception to the rule. Instead of a personal dialogue between Yahweh and Israel, Levitical worship consists of complicated, mostly silent, rituals.

That's a misperception. The book of Leviticus itself is made up almost entirely of Yahweh's words to Moses. Israel performs rites of offering, priests carry out priestly service, and Israelites observe purity regulations in response to Yahweh's word. Israel's ritual actions speak back obediently to God's speech.

Ritual is always a form of communication. A giddy young man gives a love-struck young woman a diamond ring. He's doing nothing new. He's following a ritual script repeated hundreds of millions of times across the centuries. It's old and repetitive, yet the script still shouts love, longing, and lifelong commitment.

In Leviticus, worship is still dialogue: Yahweh instructs Israel how to approach Him→Israel answers by doing what He commands→Yahweh smells the soothing aroma and is pleased. God invites Israel to His house, and Israel speaks back with acts of sacrifice, in blood, fire, and smoke.

The romantic example I gave a couple of paragraphs back isn't accidental. Yahweh is Husband to Israel. The Sinai covenant is their wedding service, and the tabernacle is their honeymoon tent. Liturgical rites maintain communion between Yahweh and His Bride.

That's what the Song of Songs is about. Modern Christians read the Song as a celebration of erotic love, and it is that. But it's *first* an allegory of Yahweh's love-play with Israel.

Temple imagery is all over the Song. The lovers' hideaway is made from cedar and cypress, the woods of the temple (SoS 1:17). The Bride is a lily (SoS 2:1), and lily designs are part of the temple décor (1 Kgs 7:19, 22, 26). The Bride is without blemish (SoS 4:7), smooth and silky as a sacrificial offering.

At the center of the poem, the lovers enter a garden to feast on one another (SoS 4:16–5:1). In this garden sanctuary, each gives him/herself to the other, just as, in the Levitical system, Israel offers herself as food to Yahweh and Yahweh gives life to His bride. The reality of mutual consumption becomes even more pronounced in the Eucharist. We're incorporated into Christ, "eaten" into His body, even as we feast on His flesh and blood. We in Him, He in us, made one flesh as Bridegroom and Bride.

Together the lovers are consumed with a love strong as death and jealous as the grave, fueled by the very flame of Yah, the flame that is Yah (SoS 8:6–7). The lovers are consumed in the sacrificial flame of Yahweh's love.

The Song's dialogues are dialogues of mutual admiration and praise. "Your love is better than wine," says the Bride (SoS 1:2). "Your love is better than wine," responds the Bridegroom (SoS 4:10). "Most beautiful among women," says the Bridegroom of his Bride (SoS 1:8). "My beloved is outstanding among ten thousand," answers the Bride (SoS 5:10). When the Bridegroom is absent, the Bride searches in desperation, willing to suffer humiliation to be restored to communion.

This *is* the liturgy. It's the liturgy of the world because the entire history of humanity is the Lord's romance with His Bride, His daring rescue that leads to a real-life, eternal happily ever after. It's the liturgy of the church, which is a dialogue of mutual admiration and praise.

The liturgy of the church encapsulates the liturgy of the world, acting it out on a small scale. The liturgy isn't a retreat from the world. It's a place and time when the dialogue of the world is done *right*, and it sets the pattern for our speech and dialogues outside the sanctuary. It's a place and time when the Bride responds in love to the Bridegroom.

We come to the door of the Lord's house, and He welcomes us with, "Come, my sister, my bride, most beautiful among women. You are altogether beautiful, without blemish, my darling, my bride." We answer with praise of our Bridegroom. "How handsome you are, beloved, and so pleasant. My beloved is like a young gazelle or stag on the mountains." We sing songs of communion: My beloved is mine, and we are His (SoS 2:16). We are our Beloved's, and He is ours (SoS 6:3). We are our Beloved's, and His desire is for us (SoS 7:10). We are mutually intoxicated by one another's love-wine, mutually consumed in the fire of Triune love.

You think liturgy is slow, repetitive, dull? It's the opposite. It's as exciting as sex. *More* exciting, since the communion of the Triune God with His Bride is the original communion of which sexual union is a copy. A splendid copy, for sure, but not the first game of love.

The upshot is plain: Wordless worship isn't *too* liturgical. Wordless worship is an *abandonment* of liturgy because Christian liturgy is a dialogue of love.

Dialogue Redeemed

Man is made in the image of the God of Scripture, and so we are communicative creatures. Yahweh places Adam in the garden to name the animals, to assign linguistic labels to other creatures. When God presents Eve to Adam, the man bursts into poetry (Gen 2:23).

From Eden on, our interactions with one another take place primarily through the medium of language. Husbands speak to wives and parents to children. Employers speak to employees, and employees talk back. Legislators write laws; judges issue decisions; kings, presidents, and prime ministers give speeches. Voters and protesters cheer or jeer in response.

Language is *the* fundamental cultural reality. Languages distinguish one group from another. The French are French because they speak to one another and name the world Frenchly. The Nuer interact Nuerly, Xhosa click the world in their Xhosan way. America and Britain are, so the quip goes, nations divided by a common language.

Language is the first common practice of every group, the one that makes all other common practices possible. Markets function only if sellers and buyers can communicate. What force can laws have if they're written in an unknown language? It's hard to get a bowling team together if bowlers don't speak the same language. If they have no language in common, each will be bowling alone.

The architect has to speak to the general contractor and the general contractor to the crew. If they can't communicate, the project will be left in ruins like Babel's unfinished tower, lonely on the plain of Shinar. Even the solitary painter in his studio has to communicate to get supplies, to present his works to buyers or museum curators, to seduce his models.

Talk is cheap, sure. But it's indispensable. Everybody's gotta talk. We can't live without it.

Our speech to one another is supposed to be a response to the speech of God. God says, "Speak truth in love" (Eph 4:15) and "Lay aside falsehood, and speak truth to your neighbor" (Eph 4:25). If we respond rightly to His word, our words to one another will build communities of truth and love, cultural habits and institutions that embody hope and justice.

But we *don't*. We don't speak rightly back to God, and so we don't speak rightly to one another.

After Adam sins, Yahweh comes to the garden to speak to him. It doesn't go well (Gen 3:8–13). Yahweh calls Adam to appear before Him, but Adam is hiding among the trees in fear and shame. Confronted with his sin, he doesn't confess, but blames Eve and ultimately blames God.

Everything's upside down. Instead of responding to a call to worship, Adam slinks out from hiding. Instead of confessing, he targets the closest scapegoat. The dialogue doesn't end with benediction but malediction, with Yahweh issuing curses against the serpent, the man, and the woman. It's the Bible's first liturgy, but it's twisted. It's an *anti*-liturgical dialogue.

When Adam's dialogue with God gets spoiled, so does his dialogue with his wife, his sons, his eventual neighbors. He submits to the serpent, whose wickedness is linguistic wickedness. Human speech becomes diabolical, full of lies, half-truths, seductions, temptations, threats, hatred, and anger. We speak like the serpent, with forked tongue.

Speech is corrupted, and so are all the common practices that rely on speech. Patterns of common life and the institutions that carry communities become infused with lies, slander, gossip, boasts, blasphemies. Husbands accuse wives instead of defending them. Parents denigrate children, and children defy parents. Sellers deceive buyers. Legislators write unjust laws, judges favor the rich or the poor, presidents and prime ministers manipulate public opinion through slick media campaigns.

The world comes under the dominion of the father of lies.

The God who creates by Word *re-creates* by Word. The eternal Word becomes flesh in order to redeem man and society. He enters our linguistic disorder to put it back in order so that our speech to God and one another is what it ought to be, restored to truth, love, hope, and justice.

Here's where the liturgy comes in. The liturgy of the church restores language so that it becomes what it's intended to be: a medium of dialogue with God and one another, the common practice that facilitates other common practices. By putting our fragmented language together again, the liturgy of the heavenly city repairs the common life of the earthly city of man.

The liturgy doesn't do this by inventing a new language. Liturgical speech isn't a religious version of Esperanto. The liturgy uses the common language of the worshiping people, which exists before it becomes a liturgical language. The Bible is translated to become a viable liturgical Bible. It uses the syntax, grammar, and vocabulary that's already there.

The church can force things. Missionaries can teach English or French to Korean, Indian, or Peruvian converts to make them worship in the missionary's tongue. That's happened often enough. But the church is called to be Pentecostal, speaking the one gospel and praising the one God in every tongue under heaven.

All human languages are broken. They've been used to lie and blaspheme. The liturgy, like the Word Himself, takes up the dilapidated language of fallen humanity. It assumes language to redeem language, so it can turn our heap of broken images into the language of Zion.

The liturgy puts an existing language to work in a new way. Pastors preach Scripture to teach people the truth about God, the world, themselves. Over years, decades, and centuries, God corrects our mis-naming and teaches His people to name the

DIALOG

world properly. The liturgy reorients existing languages so they begin to speak rightly in response to God's speech.

New vocabulary must be added: words for sin, the cross, resurrection, the heavenly city. New names are added to the stock of names: Adam, Abel, Abraham, David and Solomon, Josiah, Jeremiah, Jesus. New sentences are uttered: "God so loved the world that He gave His only Son." Converted worshipers sing and speak in *their* language to praise and thank the Creator, who is Father, Son, and Spirit. Tongues once used to praise Marduk or Zeus or Allah become instruments of righteous praise, directed to the living God.

In the liturgy, language does what language is created to do. In the liturgy, the language is redeemed and fulfilled as it's *Christianized*, infused and corrected by the Scriptures. The liturgy doesn't just *lead* to the Christianization of language. It's the first Christianization of language, which anticipates the final transformation of language in new Jerusalem, the un-Babel when people of every tongue will be united in praise to the Lord and the Lamb.

The liturgy performs this magic by the power of Word and Spirit. The church may abandon Scripture and turn her liturgy into an echo of the diabolical dialogue of the world. That doesn't redeem language but degrades it more deeply. The church can carry on the dialogue of the liturgy while defying the Spirit of the liturgy. Then the Spirit of Pentecost takes flight, and the church is just another outpost of Babelic confusion.

To redeem language, the liturgy must be reformed and refreshed, again and again. It must be called back, again and again, to Scripture. It must be carried out by people who walk in the Spirit to follow the Lord Jesus.

But a liturgy infused with Scripture performed by people filled with the Spirit—*that* is an agent for the redemption of the world. As I said in the Preface, culture is the six-day bridge between creation and eschaton. Liturgy orients culture toward its ultimate purpose. In the city of God, liturgy is the seventh-day initial transformation of culture, redirecting damaged words toward their proper end.

Divine Dialogue

Through most of the church's history, Christian worship has been just the kind of dialogue I've been describing. A priest or minister is ordained to speak Christ's word to the people, and the people respond as the Bride. You hear the minister's voice, but he doesn't speak his own words. Jesus authorizes him to speak, and the words he speaks *ought* to be the words of Jesus. The liturgy might look like a dialogue between minister and people. In reality, it's a dialogue between Bridegroom and Bride. It's the church's participation in the trialogue of Father, Son, and Spirit.

To illustrate how this works in practice, I'll run through a standard Lutheran liturgy. You can find the same dialogic patterns in Catholic, Orthodox, Anglican, Methodist, Reformed, and other liturgies. This *is* the church's historic liturgy.

Many of the specific phrases, songs, prayers don't come directly from the Bible. They could be different. But any liturgy shaped by the Bible is going to look something like this. It's going to be a dialogue between God and His people, organized around Word and Table.

The conversation begins as soon as the congregation assembles. After a procession, the minister greets the baptized people in the Lord's name: "In the Name of the Father, and of the Son, and of the Holy Spirit." The people respond with "Amen."

It's a word of welcome. It's also a word of new creation. The minister speaks the word of the eternal Word. Through him, the Word that summoned the world into existence summons the church into being. Through the minister, the Word gathers a new-created humanity in the midst of fallen humanity.

Having called us to worship, the minister calls us to confess our sins. To commune with the Bridegroom, the Bride needs to enter His presence fragrant with the fragrance of the Bridegroom. She needs to freshen up.

The call to confess is again a dialogue:[1]

> M: I said, I will confess my transgressions unto the Lord.
> C: And thou forgavest the iniquity of my sin.

Minister and people then kneel to confess their sins before God and one another, with these or similar words:

> Almighty God, our Maker and Redeemer, we poor sinners confess unto thee, that we are by nature sinful and unclean, and that we have sinned against thee by thought, word, and deed. Wherefore we flee for refuge to thine infinite mercy, seeking and imploring thy grace, for the sake of our Lord Jesus Christ.

Notice what's happening here: English is being used to admit our sin and disobedience before a holy God. A language that was already in development before the gospel arrived is deployed to express humble contrition. Every time an English-speaking congregation confesses sin, it contributes to the redemption of the language and moves the world toward its final glory.

After confession, the minister pronounces absolution; that is, he assures the people that their sins are, in fact, forgiven:

> Arise and hear the good news! Brothers and sisters who have been baptized into union with Jesus Christ, God Himself promises you the forgiveness of the Father, the victory of the Son, and the glory and empowerment of the Holy Spirit. Believe this, and rejoice.

---

[1] In the following, "M" stands for "Minister" and "C" for "Congregation."

Remember, this *isn't* the minister's promise. It's not his opinion. He speaks for the Son, who speaks the words the Father gives Him. When the minister says, "Your sins are forgiven," you should take it as God's address to you. Don't trust the minister. Trust God.

And rejoice. After the people respond with an "Amen," the liturgy kicks into high gear with a series of sung responses. The *Kyrie Eleison* ("Lord, have mercy"), the *Gloria in Excelsis* ("Glory in the highest," an ancient hymn of praise), the *Te Deum* ("We praise you, O God") together constitute an ascension in song.

Having humbled ourselves in confession, the Lord raises us to glory. We climb the heavenly Zion to join angels and saints in joyful assembly (Heb 12:18–24). Heaven and earth join in a universal dialogue in God's cosmic house. We anticipate the final Zion, when there will be no words but words of praise. Filled with praise, the church is the heavenly city, present now in part with hope for a future fullness.

One of the traditional dialogues is the *Kyrie*, a Trinity-shaped set of petitions and pleas for mercy. A simple version is

> M: Lord, have mercy upon us.
> C: Lord have mercy upon us.
> M: Christ, have mercy upon us.
> C: Christ, have mercy upon us.
> M: Lord, have mercy upon us.
> C: Lord, have mercy upon us.

Sometimes the *Kyrie* is more elaborate:

> M: In peace let us pray to the Lord.
> C: Lord, have mercy.
> M: For the peace that is from above, and for the salvation of our souls, let us pray to the Lord.
> C: Lord, have mercy.
> M: For the peace of the whole world, for the well-being of the

churches of God, and for the unity of all, let us pray to the Lord.
C: Lord, have mercy.
M: For this holy house, and for them that in faith, piety, and fear of God offer here their worship and praise, let us pray to the Lord.
C: Lord, have mercy.
M: Help, save, pity and defend us, O God, by thy grace.
C: Amen.

The minister has conducted us from the foot of the mountain to the peak. Using the keys of the kingdom, he's unlocked the door of the Lord's house and led us into the inner chamber, where the most intense communion happens. Every step has been a small dialogue setting up for the climactic dialogue in preaching, prayer, and feasting.

Churches have traditionally introduced corporate prayers with a snippet of dialogue:

M: The Lord be with you.
C: And with thy spirit.

It's a small gesture, but profound. With this exchange, minister and people form a communion of prayer in the Spirit. Through the Spirit, in fact, minister and people enter the communion of the Triune God. The church's dialogue is folded into the eternal conversation of love that is Triune life.

Formed by the Word

At the mountaintop, the Lord speaks directly to us in readings from the Bible. Many churches use "lectionaries," an annual cycle of Scripture readings. Each week, the lectionary prescribes an Old Testament, an Epistle, and a Gospel reading.

Each reading corresponds to the season of the church year. During Advent, Old Testament readings are prophecies of the Messiah or the new covenant. Epistle readings are prophecies of the Lord's coming or the final judgment. Gospel readings include Jesus' Palm Sunday entry to Jerusalem, Jesus' Olivet Discourse (Matt 24), or narratives about the incarnation. Through the lectionary, the dialogue of the liturgy is tuned to the time of redemption, the life, death, and resurrection of Jesus the Messiah.

At the end of each reading, the minister says, "The word of the Lord," and the congregation responds with gratitude: "Thanks be to God." Another small but profound gesture. God often speaks to comfort and give hope. But His word is also a sword (Heb 4:11–12). His word breaks into our hearts to dig up hidden sins and bring them to light. He speaks terrifying judgments that chill the bones. And yet, *no matter what word He speaks*, no matter how shattering or startling, the liturgy trains the church to say, "Thank you." It's more than etiquette. It's a confession of faith: Even when He kills us, God intends good. He intends to raise us to new life.

This is another moment in the redemption of language and culture. God initiates the dialogue of history and of the liturgy. Our response should always be grateful obedience. Often, it's grumbling disobedience. Here, at least—here in the liturgy—we say what we should when God speaks. We say, "Thank you."

Sunday's "Thank you" sets the tone for the rest of the week. When God speaks in the world, in the midst of difficulties in family or at work, in the midst of our doubts and fears, we repeat Sunday's "Thank you." Thus the liturgical dialogue reshapes the dialogic patterns of daily life.

When we don't, when we grumble or close our ears, Sunday's "Thank you" stands in judgment. We go back to church the following week, again hear God's word, again say, "Thanks be to God." If we're paying attention, it should be a moment of self-examination and repentance. Sunday's "Thank you" is the measure of our everyday speech in the dialogue of life. Sunday's "Thank you" in the heavenly city tests our speech in the earthly city.

In the sermon, the minister speaks the Lord's word more pointedly to a specific congregation. If he's doing his job, he'll stick to the text. He shouldn't be telling stories or commenting on the World Cup. He should be delivering the word of God to the people of God. Through the readings and preaching, the word comes into its own. The written text becomes a living voice. Through the text read and taught, the Spirit of Jesus speaks to the churches (cf. Rev 2–3).[2]

There's a lot of talk these days about "formation" and about the liturgy's role in forming virtuous men and women. Scripture teaches the liturgy is formative, but in a more direct way. We're deformed because we worship idols. We need to be formed into worshipers. That's what the liturgy does. If it conforms to God's will for worship, it's an act of true worship, and those who participate are worshipers.

Everyone who participates in Christian liturgy worships the true God. They pray to the Father of Jesus, praise the Triune God, hear the word of God, and gather at the table of Jesus Christ.

Of course, not everyone who participates in the Christian liturgy worships the true God *truly*. Some are cunning conscious hypocrites. Some desperately doubt. Some are more devoted to idols than to the true God. Done rightly, done biblically, the liturgy shatters false worshipers to raise them up as true worshipers. The liturgy is the work of the Triune God. It's the Father's work on us by His two hands, the Son and Spirit. Through the acts,

---

[2] I have written about preaching in the first volume in this series, *The Theopolitan Vision*, 77–80.

gestures, words, and rhythms of the liturgy, the Spirit is calling us into fellowship. Through the liturgy, God is making worshipers.

It's especially through the word that the liturgy makes worshipers. Husbands who spend the week abusing their wives hear Paul's words: "Husbands, love your wives as Christ loved the church" (Eph 5:22-33). Children who resent their parents hear God say, "Children, obey your parents" (Eph 6:1). Employers who abuse their employees are confronted by the Torah's demands for justice. Slumlords who prosper on the suffering of the poor hear the severe words of Isaiah: I hate your new moons. Stop this trampling of my courts. Your hands are covered with blood (Isa 1).

Suppose they hear all this and *still* don't change? Even then the Spirit works on them, convicting them of sin, righteousness, and judgment (John 16:5-8). No one can participate in a faithful Christian liturgy without being formed like clay into a worshiper or hardened into a brittle vessel that will eventually be shattered. No one walks out unchanged.

As I've said before, this happens only when the liturgy is thoroughly biblical, saturated with Scripture. Worship forms worshipers only if they are confronted by the word, sing the word, dialogue in the word, eat and drink the Word at the Lord's table.

Lack of emphasis on the word has been one of the glaring weaknesses of "liturgical churches." They have pomp and ritual and sacrament and mystery. They have awesome cathedrals and chapels. They have colorful vestments, pungent aromas, transcendent choral music.

Without the word at the center, none of this is effective. Wordless liturgy can form aesthetes. It can make traditionalists. It can make Pharisees. It *can't* make worshipers who carry on the liturgy of life in faith. It can't do what the liturgy is intended to do—redeem language and redirect it toward the new creation. I'll repeat myself: The problem with "liturgical churches" isn't that they're *too* liturgical. Insofar as they sideline the word, they aren't liturgical enough, for the liturgy *is* God speaking to and feeding His people.

Love Feast

Traditionally, the Eucharist also begins with a series of exchanges between minister and people. Bridegroom and Bride speak words of love as they approach their love feast and their marriage supper:

> M: The Lord be with you.
> C: And with thy spirit.
> M: Lift up your hearts.
> C: We lift them up to the Lord.
> M: Let us give thanks to the Lord our God.
> C: It is meet, proper, and right so to do.

Once again, minister and people form a communion of prayer in the Spirit prior to the Eucharistic thanksgiving. In the *Sursum Corda* ("Lift up your hearts"), the church acknowledges it ascends to heaven for the communion meal. By giving thanks, the church acknowledges it's a moment of "Eucharist," thanksgiving.

Of course, the Eucharist isn't our only moment of thanks. The liturgy of thanks expresses the church's culture of gratitude. "In everything give thanks," Paul says (1 Thess 5:18). And again, "always give thanks for all things" (Eph 5:20). Saying thanks at the Lord's table trains us to receive *everything* with thanks (1 Tim 4:4–5).

We're inclined to grumble. Complaint becomes habitual. Ingratitude is institutionalized in media, political, educational systems devoted to critique. Contemporary culture is designed to foster discontent. The Eucharistic liturgy challenges cultural habits and institutions and infuses the lives of Christians and churches with perpetual thanks. It Christianizes culture by filling our mouths with the words of God: "O give thanks to the Lord, for He is good" (Pss 106:1; 107:1).

This dialogue marks off the Eucharist from the prior "liturgy of the word." That distinction can go wrong. It might lead us to think there are two liturgies, one where the Lord *speaks* and the other where He *feeds* us. We might think that He speaks on earth, and we ascend only when we come to the Lord's table.

Many liturgies give that impression. The liturgy of the word is detachable as a self-standing service. Some churches do a Eucharistic liturgy only on special occasions. That's a mistake. There's only one liturgy, a liturgy of Word-and-Table, a liturgy of communion in Word and food. And after the confession and absolution, the whole liturgy takes place on the mountaintop, in heavenly places.

Every Sunday is a feast day. Every Lord's Day is Eucharistic. Every Sunday, liturgy should be a liturgy of Word *and* Sacrament. God's people have always worshiped at tables. So should we.

To avoid the idea of divided service, it's best to move the *Sursum Corda* to the beginning of the liturgy, right after the confession and absolution. That way, it'll be clear that the word is a heavenly word, just as the table is a heavenly table. Churches that keep the *Sursum Corda* in its traditional place need to make it clear that the liturgy isn't divided and that the whole service occurs in heavenly places. The whole liturgy, from the call to worship through the Eucharist, is a single divine dialogue.

God has spoken. The Father has spoken words about the Word through the Spirit. God has fed us. The Father has given us the body and blood of His Son through the Spirit. Now God is ready to let us go. He speaks one final word, the "good word" of Benediction, ending the service with the same Triune name that began the service:

The Lord bless you and guard you.
The Lord make His face to shine upon you and be gracious to you.
The Lord lift up His countenance upon you and give you His peace.
In the Name of the Father, and of the Son, and of the Holy Spirit. Amen.

The liturgy anticipates the final order of things. The liturgical dialogue puts our dislocated language right. In the liturgy, we hear God's word afresh and respond the way we ought to respond, with loving thanks. But the liturgy doesn't stand alone. The liturgy of the church sets the standard for the liturgy of the world. The dialogue of worship needs to shape the dialogue of our lives, society, politics, and culture. Having spoken right speech with the gathered city of God, we're to speak rightly when we return to the city of man.

Conclusion

God speaks. That's a wonderful thing. He's not silent. He's not left us in the dark about His plans or His demands. He lets us know what's on His mind. He doesn't tell us everything, of course. But He tells us everything we need to know.

God speaks, and God is *spoken to*. That's *also* a wonderful thing. We can imagine a God who is so austere, so transcendent, that He cannot be approached or addressed. He'd be like the unknown god of the Athenians (Acts 17). They know he's there, but they don't know anything about him. They can't be sure he hears their prayers or receives smoke signals from their altars.

God is spoken-*to* because God's life is an eternal conversation of Father, Son, and Spirit. In the Trinity, God is the speaking God, the Father who utters the Word in the Spirit. In the Trinity, God is the spoken-to God, the Word who speaks back to the Father in the Spirit.

Dialogue is the shape of Christian worship because the liturgy conforms to God's own life. It's the shape of Christian liturgy because the liturgy takes place *within* the Triune life, as the body of the Son hears the word of the Father and speaks back in the Son.

When it is a dialogue in the Word, carried out by a people walking with the Spirit, the dialogic structure of worship forms a communion of worshipers, a liturgical city. More profoundly, it forms a communion between the worshipers and the Worshiped. Thus the Lord uses the liturgy to redeem our twisted languages and transform them into the language of the kingdom.

3   SACRIFICE

God . . . separated the waters which were below the expanse from the waters which were above the expanse . . .
Genesis 1:7

Pop quiz: Who offers the first sacrifice in the Bible?

If you answered "Cain" or "Abel," you're awfully close. But close isn't the same as right. There's a sacrifice before Cain and Abel were even born. In fact, there are several. These are easy to miss, but they're essential for understanding the purpose and shape of biblical sacrifice.

Glorification by Sacrifice

In Genesis 1, God judges things "good" seven times (Gen 1:4, 10, 12, 18, 21, 25, 31). More good things appear in Genesis 2—the fruit of the trees in the garden (2:9) and the gold of the land of Havilah (2:12).

Just when we're getting into the rhythm, He suddenly shifts gears. "It is *not* good" (Gen 2:18). The thing that's not good is Adam's solitariness. Why does it matter if Adam is alone? Why is *that* the one not-good thing in creation?

We might think Adam needs a friend. But God is with him, offering all the friendship he could hope for. We might think that Adam needs help to fulfill his mission. That's true, but he can carry out a lot of his work of dominion using his own muscles and training animals.

One thing he *can't* do without another human: Be fruitful and multiply. Adam alone is Adam fruitless. Alone, Adam can't reproduce or fill the earth. As God designed the world, another male human won't do the trick either. Adam isn't biologically equipped to be fruitful on his own. Double Adam, triple Adam, keep adding Adams until there's an unimaginable number of Adams, and they still won't be fruitful. Guys with guys can't make more guys.

Adam needs a helper who "corresponds" to him (Gen 2:18). That helper has to be like him but can't be *exactly* like him. To multiply, Adam needs another human who is similar with a difference. He's a man and needs a woman. Or, in the original Hebrew, he's an *'ish* who needs an *'ishshah*.

Reproduction is one important reason why Adam needs a partner. But it's not the most basic reason. Remember chapter 1, where I said the garden is the original human *sanctuary*, the "holy place" where God meets with Adam, where they converse and where Adam is supposed to eat in the presence of God. When Yahweh says, "It's not good for man to be alone," He's talking about the *garden*: "It's not good for Adam to be alone, *in the sanctuary*." Adam does need a partner to multiply and fill the earth. He also needs a partner for worship. He needs a *liturgical* helper.

Once we see that this is the issue in Genesis 2, the rest of the story takes on fresh meaning. Adam inspects the animals, but none is a "helper corresponding to him." For a long time, animals serve as mediators in Israel's worship. But from the beginning, it is not so. Yahweh gives Adam a *human* partner so they can commune with the Creator.

Remember how God makes that human partner? Adam doesn't find her among the animals. Yahweh doesn't dig into the ground and mold a woman, as He molds Adam. Instead, Yahweh puts Adam into deep sleep, a death-like, coma-slumber. While Adam is asleep, the Lord removes a rib and builds a woman from the rib. When Adam wakes up, he knows he's found his helper. He recognizes her as a sister: "bone of my bone, flesh of my flesh" (Gen 2:21–23).

There it is! *That's* the sacrifice. Did you miss it? Let me go through it more slowly.

Adam is put into a state near death, and his body is divided in two. That's what happens to animals offered on the altar. They're slaughtered, and their bodies are dismembered. (The other man put into "death-sleep" is Abram, who has a vision after dividing animals to cut covenant with Yahweh [Gen 15].)

For Adam, division isn't the end of the story. Adam is divided into two pieces, but the final aim is to reunite as "one flesh" with the woman made from his rib (Gen 2:24). He's divided in two in order to enter a higher state of unity.

"The woman," Paul says, "is the glory of the man" (1 Cor 11:7). Proverbs speaks of an excellent wife as a crown to her husband, raising him to royalty (Prov 12:4). Adam passes through death and dismemberment to be glorified. He "dies" in order to rise in a new form. He dies and rises to become king.

That's what sacrifice *always* does. We moderns rarely see an animal butchered. We think meat is naturally shrink-wrapped, ready for the shelves. It can be traumatic for us to see an animal slaughtered. We can't get past the violence.

That's not the focus of biblical sacrifice. Of course, the animal dies, as Adam "dies" in the garden. But that's only one first moment of sacrifice. Sacrifice is a pathway, a *movement* through death to new life. In sacrifice, we die to one state so we can rise in an exalted state. Adam is a seed that must go into the ground to die before it can bear fruit (John 12:24). So are we.

Notice: This early sacrifice isn't an animal sacrifice. It's a *human* sacrifice, the death-and-division of Adam to become a new and improved man, Adam-and-Eve. That sets a trajectory toward the final sacrifice, the death of Jesus on the cross, which brings forth a new Eve, the church, from His spear-pierced ribs (John 19:34).

Once we see sacrifice in Genesis 2, we can see how sacrifice is built into the structures of creation and undergirds history. Adam's surgery isn't the first sacrifice. *Creation* is a sacrificial procedure.

To form the world, Yahweh divides light and darkness and choreographs them in a dance of day and night. He separates the waters above and below and divides the waters below to form dry land. He separates a portion of the earth (*'adamah*) to form an *'adam*. At every stage, it's division-and-reunion. The creation week is a week of sacrifice.

History moves in sacrificial rhythms. God wipes out the world in the flood, sends Noah through death-waters in a coffin-ark so that he can rise as a new Adam doing Godlike, royal things—planting a vineyard, confronting his son Ham (as Yahweh confronted his son Adam), declaring curses (Gen 9:20–27).

Yahweh tears Israel from Egypt, leads them through the Red Sea, and brings them to Sinai where He elevates them to be His royal priesthood. He tears Israel from the land, sends them to the grave of exile, then raises them up (cf. Ezek 37) into a new and better covenant (Jer 31).

This is *your* life too. You started life in the cozy comfort of your mother's womb, but then you got squeezed out, screaming. You died to the womb to come alive in the world. Then you had your first day of school, your first date, your wedding, your first child, your first grandchild, the death of your mother and father. Each of these crisis moments is a small death that shatters the world as you know it. If life carries on at all, it carries on with a new, unknown horizon. No wonder life can be terrifying. You're constantly dying to *this* to come alive to *that*.

You *live* sacrifice. You live it *every day*, and so does the world. Each day descends into the darkness of night, into sleep, death's second self, until morning breaks like the first morning, the blackbird speaks like the first dawn, and you wake to a new creation.

Division to reunion, death to resurrection, grave to glory—that's the way the world comes to be and the way the world works. It's the sacrificial movement of creation, life, and history. Sacrificial liturgy doesn't introduce an alien pattern into the world. It runs along the grain of a sacrificial cosmos.

Covering

Creation, including the creation of Eve, constitutes the first and foundational sacrifice. But there's another sacrifice in the first chapters of the Bible. And it brings out other essential dimensions of sacrifice and liturgical life.

After Adam and Eve eat the fruit of the tree of knowledge, they recognize they're naked and sew fig leaf aprons to cover their shame (Gen 3:7). Those aren't effective coverings. They're as lame as Adam's excuses and blame-shifting.

Adam and Eve can't provide covering for themselves. God has to give covering, and He does. He provides animal skins (Gen 3:21). In order to get animal skins, Yahweh has to kill and skin some animals. How appropriate: The Lord performs this first post-fall sacrifice as He offers the final sacrifice, the self-sacrifice of the Lamb.

What can we learn from this first animal offering?

Sacrifice produces a covering. That's what the word "atone" means (Heb. *kaphar*). To make atonement is to cover. Why do

Adam and Eve need covering? Adam and Eve want protective covering. They don't want to be exposed naked before the Lord. They don't want their shame displayed. Sacrifice covers sin, so sinners can appear in the presence of God without shame. Sacrifice covers us, so we don't have to cower among the trees of the garden. Like Jacob, we come to our Father wearing the skin of the Firstborn so that we can receive His blessing (cf. Gen 27).

Animal coverings represent a demotion. Adam and Eve listen to the voice of a serpent rather than the voice of the Lord. They obey a beast, and so they're clothed like beasts. They serve the creature and descend into animality. But there's a plus side. Clothing marks identity and status. Priests and kings wear robes. Prophets like Elijah and John the Baptist were known for their distinctive clothing. Covered with "vestments," we're "invested" with prestige. Coverings cover. Coverings also *glorify*.

Sacrifice has both of these effects at once. On the one hand, it covers our sin and shame and makes us acceptable to God. On the other hand, it installs us as priests and kings. Adam leaves the garden robed in an animal skin because he is the forgiven prince of creation, son of the Creator King.

There's more about sacrifice in Genesis 3. After Adam and Eve are expelled from the garden, Yahweh sets cherubim at the eastern gate, armed with flaming swords to prevent Adam's return to the tree of life (3:24). The message is clear: If you want to eat the fruit of the tree of life, you'll have to slip past the cherubim. They're hard to slip past. Cherubim are full of eyes, watching in every direction all the time (Ezek 1:18; 10:12). Try slipping past *that*.

If you're *really* determined to get back to Eden, you can try another tack: Charge straight for the gate. That plan doesn't pass the cost-benefit analysis. If you charge the gate of Eden, the cherubim will swing their fiery swords, and you'll be cut into stew meat and turned to smoke. There's no way to survive.

SACRIFICE

You'll hesitate to charge the gate unless you're pretty confident you'll rise from the dead on the other side.

Those cherubim represent a problem. Inside Eden are all God's gifts. He offers life. He offers the wisdom of the tree of knowledge. *He* is present. In Eden, you can find all the treasures later deposited in the ark—food, word, a shepherd. The only catch is that you can't get in without being killed. Stay out, and you can't get to the tree of life. So you die. Try to get in, and cherubim kill you. So you die. It looks pretty hopeless.

Sacrifice is the solution to that dilemma. Sacrifice is the Lord's gracious alternative to the choice between the certain death of exclusion and the certain death of re-entry. Sacrifice enables us to enter the garden to enjoy its gifts. Sacrifice assures you you'll live again after passing by the cherubim.

Instead of being left out in the grave, instead of being cut down by cherubim, you can send in an animal substitute. By entering the altar, the animal goes through Eden's gate, suffers the cherubic sword and fire, and ascends as soothing aroma to Yahweh.

Sacrifice is a gate liturgy. Sacrifice is the ritual path of return. Sacrifice cuts a way through death to glorified new life. Through sacrifice, we can return to God in what the Bible speaks of as a "covenant," a committed union of love. In the garden, Adam "dies" and rises to a new life. Outside the garden, sacrifice enables his children to experience the same progress from glory to glory.

There's one last thing we learn about sacrifice from Genesis 3. We return to the garden to *eat* in the presence of God. Sacrifice is a gate liturgy, and the gate is the entry to a banquet hall. Sacrifice is a *food* rite.

That's actually implied by the Hebrew verb for "sacrifice," *zavach*. It means specifically "to slaughter for a meal" or "to butcher." Whenever the Old Testament uses the term "sacrifice," it implies a feast.

To say biblical worship is sacrificial is to say that it takes place at a table. *All* worship in the Bible takes place at a table. In the old world, Israel worships at altar-tables where animals are turned to smoke. Now in the heavenly city, we gather at the Lord's table where the Father gives us the body and blood of His Son through the Spirit. Biblically speaking, worship without a meal isn't worship at all. It's missing the crucial piece of furniture—a table—and the crucial liturgical materials—bread and wine.

What have we learned about sacrifice from Genesis 1–3?

- Sacrificial division and reunion, death and resurrection, are built into creation.
- Sacrifice is a movement of glorification by death-and-resurrection.
- Before there are animal sacrifices, there's a *human* sacrifice—Adam put into death-sleep to produce a bride. Human sacrifice is the original, and the final, form of sacrifice.
- Sacrifice covers, covering shame and conferring glory. By covering, it allows us to enter the presence of God.
- A worshiper enters the presence of God through a substitute who suffers death on his behalf.
- Once in the presence of God, worshipers eat and drink and rejoice together. The sacrificial substitute gives himself as food for a feast.

Everything else the Bible teaches about sacrifice—the complex Levitical system of offerings, the sacrifice of Jesus, the sacrificial praise of the temple and the church—all of it builds on the foundation of Genesis 1–3.

Above all, everything else the Bible teaches about sacrifice builds on this basic truth: *God* performs the first sacrifices, and He does it to glorify the creation and to cover and glorify us. In that, we already see the gospel because the God who performs the first sacrifice also offers the last. God is the Alpha and Omega of sacrifice.

Sacrifice Before Sinai

God creates by sacrifice. He forms Eve and the union of man-and-woman by sacrifice. Made in the image of this God, human beings are sacrificial creatures. Along with place, language, and time, sacrifice is one of the constants of human life. We reshape a sacrificial creation into sacrificial culture.

Ancient peoples performed various rites of animal or human sacrifice. Every ancient Greek home had its hearth fire not only for cooking but for domestic sacrifice. Temples were built on the central acropolis of ancient Greek cities, houses for the gods and places for sacrificial festivity.

Ancient political life was infused with sacrifice. The Greek citizen assembly was called to order by the sacrifice of a pig. If a city established a colony, it would carry sacred fire from the home city to light the hearth fire of the new city, because a city couldn't be a city without a place for civic sacrifice.

Romans offered sacrifices before battles and to celebrate victories. Shakespeare knew his Romans. His Julius Caesar asks a priest to examine the entrails of an animal before he enters the Senate on the day of his assassination. It's just the thing superstitious emperors did.

When Yahweh instructs Israel to offer animals on altars, He doesn't invent a new custom. It's already pervasive. From Egypt to Babylon and Assyria, from China and Persia to the Inca and Mayan empires, sacrifice was a central rite of all ancient civilizations. All of them were children of Adam and Noah and continued the sacrificial customs of Eden and Ararat.

But God isn't accommodating to human custom. Ultimately, ancient peoples sacrifice because they're children of a sacrificial Creator, who baked sacrifice into the bread of creation. As we have seen throughout this book, culture reflects and builds on the patterns of creation, whether faithfully or unfaithfully.

Since Adam's sin, cultures build defectively, perversely. In most ancient cultures, sacrifices are offered to false gods, what Paul describes as "demons" (1 Cor 10:20). Idolatrous sacrifices offer false paths to life, atonements that are no better than fig leaves. They don't enhance life, but destroy it.

Yahweh instructs Israel how to sacrifice to redeem this universal cultural practice. In Israel's sacrificial liturgy, He redirects sacrifice back to its true end— glorification, entry into Eden, covering and communion with the living God.

True and false sacrifices appear together early in the Bible, in the account of Cain and Abel (Gen 4). For Cain and Abel, sacrifice is a gate liturgy. They are born outside Eden, and they can't draw near to God without being cut down by the cherubim. They bring their offerings near to send a substitute past the angelic guardians.

We typically have a childish, Sunday-school idea of what happens between Cain and Abel. We imagine two teenagers who each build an altar and make a solitary offering. It's much more likely they perform their sacrifices in public. Nearly all sacrifices in the Bible are public events. Abram sets up altars all over the land of promise to lead his company of perhaps a thousand men, women, and children in worship (with 318 fighting men, Gen 14:14). All of Israel's sacrifices take place in public at the altar of the sanctuary.

We should imagine Cain and Abel doing the same. Cain approaches the gate of Eden with his company of worshipers. Abel gathers his clan in the same location. When Abel brings his animal near, the cherubim send out fire that consumes the offering, a sign that Yahweh accepts it. Cain sets out his vegetable offering, but there's no fire.

That's why Cain becomes angry, envious, ultimately murderous. He's been publicly shamed, and by his kid brother. God acknowledges Abel but not Cain, and *everybody knows it*.

SACRIFICE

Cain is the first murderer. Before he's a murderer, though, he's a false worshiper. His hatred arises from a conflict over worship. We think politics are the source of history's wars. In fact, liturgy is the secret core of political history.

Why does God accept Abel's offering but not Cain's? Abel offers animals, imitating Yahweh's first offering. Cain, a "servant of the ground," offers vegetable offerings. Later, Israel offers grain offerings, but they're always *added* to animal offerings. One of the lessons of the first sacrifice is this: Without the shedding of blood, there's no atonement (Heb 9:22). Blood alone *covers*.

There's another reason. Every ritual has what Dru Johnson calls a "biography." The ritual isn't just what happens at the sanctuary. It includes the whole backstory of how the worshiper acquires the offering, how he lives outside the sanctuary, how he treats his wife and children and employees and parents on the day of sacrifice.

If a worshiper steals a neighbor's lamb for an offering, Yahweh doesn't accept it. Even if the animal is without blemish and the worshiper goes through the right liturgical motions, the offering is tainted. God evaluates the offering on the basis of its entire "biography."

You can't bring an acceptable offering if your hands are filled with innocent blood (Isa 1:1–18). Your offering is tainted if you abuse your employees or ignore the needs of the hungry, naked, homeless, and poor. You can't pretend your offering expresses love for God if you spend your life hating your brother. Acts of sacrificial worship can't be disconnected from the whole life of the worshiper. Israel repeatedly forgets this. They think they can cover evil lives with a blood-and-smoke screen of sacrifice. Yahweh sees right through it and sends prophets like Jeremiah to condemn it (Jer 7).

God doesn't accept Cain's offering because it isn't liturgically correct. More important, the Lord rejects his offering because he hates his brother (1 John 3:10–12).

Sacrifice of Kings

Noah is the next person to make an offering. After the flood, he sets up an altar and offers all kinds of clean animals. Yahweh smells the soothing aroma and promises never to curse the ground again (Gen 8:20–22).

This is new. Both Cain and Abel offered *minchah* offerings (Gen 4:3–4). A *minchah* is "tribute," homage from an inferior to a superior. Subject kings bring *minchah* to their overlords. Noah offers an *'olah*. The Hebrew word means "to go up," and the offering represents ascension. For the first time, we learn that sacrifice "ascends" into the Lord's presence as an *aroma*.

Noah's *'olah* also tells us something about Noah. Yahweh has undone creation, turning it back into a formless and watery void (cf. Gen 1:2). Noah emerges from the ark like Adam from the ground, head of a new human race, a second Adam, called to multiply, fill, and rule the earth (Gen 9:7).

But Noah doesn't go back to the starting blocks. He's a new and *improved* Adam. Unlike Adam, he's allowed to eat flesh (Gen 9:3–4). Unlike Adam, he has authority to punish evildoers (Gen 9:5–7). Yahweh planted the first garden and set Adam in it. Noah plants his *own* garden, a vineyard, and enjoys the first wine (Gen 9:20–21). Having gone through the sacrificial death-and-elevation of the flood, Noah naturally presents "elevation" offerings.

Yahweh intends for Adam to become a king. But Adam fails as a priest, and his path to kingship is blocked. The children of Cain become kings, but they're brutal tyrants who fill the earth with violence (Gen 4:16–24). It takes another creation, and another Adam, for a righteous king to appear on earth. Noah offers ascension offerings because *he* has ascended. He offers ascension offerings to acknowledge there's a higher, heavenly King.

Yahweh's sacrifice in Eden produces coverings. Noah's ascension offering produces an aroma (Gen 8:21). When Yahweh gets angry, the Hebrew Bible says his "nose burns." By turning an animal to smoke, Noah calms Yahweh's burning nose. The ascension offering "covers" God's anger. It covers Noah, so he bears the aroma of the substitute (cf. 2 Cor 2:14).

When Yahweh smells the aroma of the ascension, He makes a covenant with Noah and, through Noah, with the world (Gen 9:8–17). He promises never to curse the ground again and to maintain the cycles of time—days and nights and seasons (Gen 8:22). Yahweh maintains the order and movement of creation in response to Noah's offering. Yahweh makes a covenant pledge in response to sacrifice. Throughout the Old Testament, He renews His covenant when He smells the fragrance of Israel's sacrifices. Sacrifice restores the covenant relation between Yahweh and His creation. Sacrificial liturgy is a liturgy of covenant-cutting and covenant-renewal.

When Noah ascends through the sacrificial animal, Yahweh promises a world at peace. As his name promises, Noah brings rest to the world (Gen 5:29) and anticipates another King who will ascend to Sabbath glory as Prince of Peace.

Liturgical Conquest

Noah is born in the tenth generation from Adam. Abram is born in the tenth generation from the second Adam, Noah. Both reboot the human race. Noah starts the human race over again after the rest are wiped out. Through Abram, Yahweh begins to renew the human race from within after the nations are scattered from Babel. Both renew the human race through sacrificial liturgy.

Noah is the first man to erect an altar, a miniature holy mountain where he communes with God. Abram builds altars everywhere he goes (Gen 12:7–8; 13:4, 18; 22:9), setting a pattern for his son Isaac, who builds an altar and digs a well (26:25).

Abram dies before he receives his inheritance, the land of promise. But as a sojourner, he consecrates the land as a place of worship. He leaves a liturgical trail from Shechem to Bethel to Ai, locations of Joshua's later conquests. He offers sacrifices from stones piled in the land so that Joshua can later offer Jericho as a civic ascension offering.

This is the sequence: First Abram makes the land a place of worship, then Yahweh hands it to his descendants. It's still the sequence for the church: Missionaries don't grab power when they enter a mission field. They start with a liturgy of word and sacrament and worship in faith until the Lord gives the land.

The first redemption of a land or nation takes place in the liturgy, and from there it radiates to the polity. Liturgy isn't a retreat from mission or political combat. Liturgy lays the foundation for mission and is on the front lines of the church's war. Liturgy is the first form of the heavenly city, the first redemption of a land or a people.

Like Noah, Abraham offers an ascension offering, on Mount Moriah (Gen 22:2–3, 6–8, 13). Initially, Isaac is the offering, but at the last minute, Yahweh intervenes to substitute a ram. Like Noah, Abraham ascends to kingship. Elevated by his obedience to God's command, he becomes a great father by his willingness to offer his son. Because of his obedience, the Lord confirms he will inherit the land and become the father of kings.

Later at Sinai, Yahweh lays out detailed instructions for the *'olah*, the ascension offering. He tells Israelites to bring a "son of the herd" (Lev 1:5). Every worshiper is an Abraham, offering a substitute son on the altar. Abraham's offering is the background for Passover, where Israelites offer lambs or goats as substitutes for their firstborn sons. By enacting the liturgy of the *'olah*, a worshiper is incorporated into the history of Abraham and Exodus. The ritual realizes a past event in the present and points toward the future.

Abraham gives up his son and receives him back, resurrected (Heb 11:19). Abraham offers his future to Yahweh, and it comes back to him renewed. Those who wish to save their future will lose it. Those who lose their future for Jesus' sake will find it. Sacrifice to the living God is an act of radical discipleship, a giving-up in hope of getting-back, a passage through death to new life.

Abraham makes his offerings among nations that have their own forms of sacrifice. His sacrificial liturgy is a moment of true sacrifice in a world filled with idols. At Abraham's altar, sacrifice is done the way sacrifice ought to be done: as worship of the true God, the God of creation and covenant, who covers sin and raises His faithful worshipers to thrones.

Sacrifice Under Torah

"Where there is a change of priesthood, there is also a change of law" (Heb 7:12). In Hebrews 7, "law" means "rule for priestly succession." The writer is talking about the change from old to new covenant. The Aaronic priests qualify for priesthood by "flesh," by birth into the line of Aaron. Jesus becomes priest by resurrection, by the power of an indestructible life.

But the principle of Hebrews is broader. The law of succession isn't the only thing that changes. The laws of worship change too. Every time there's a change of priesthood, there's a liturgical revolution.

That's what happens when Israel arrives at Sinai. There's a change in priesthood, and the liturgy receives a radical makeover.

Prior to Sinai, there is no special caste of priests. Noah, Abram, Isaac, and others serve at altars. Perhaps their sons assist.

After the exodus, Yahweh chooses Aaron and his sons to serve at the altar and to keep His house. They offer Yahweh's bread on His altar-table. They trim the wicks of the lamps and refill them with oil so the light doesn't go out in Israel. They burn the incense of prayer. They bear the sins and impurities of Israel so that they can be removed on the Day of Atonement. They guard the sanctuary from intruders.

Priests are servants of Yahweh's royal house, and Yahweh chooses Aaron as priest at the same time He instructs Israel to build a house where He will dwell in glory.

Abram entertains angels, including the Angel of Yahweh. But the Angel of Yahweh doesn't move into Abram's neighborhood. At Sinai, Yahweh does just that. Israel lives in tents in the wilderness, and in the middle of their camp is Yahweh's tent. For the first time since Eden, human beings live in proximity to the Creator.

And, for the first time since the fall, human beings slip past the cherubim. They can't go *all* the way in. Lay Israelites have to stay in the courtyard, and priests are limited to the Holy Place. But the Lord's house is nearby, and He opens it for hospitality, for eating, drinking, and rejoicing (Deut 12:1–7).

If God comes close, you can't just keep up business as usual. Israel's liturgy has to change. Because Yahweh is close, Israel has to be concerned about purity. Normal bodily processes suddenly become dangerous.

- Certain meats become unclean (Lev 11).
- Women are unclean after childbirth (Lev 12).
- People with skin disease are unclean, and so are mildewed clothing and houses (Lev 13–14).
- Men become unclean because of genital emissions, and women are unclean during their menstrual periods (Lev 15).
- Even within marriage, sex makes both man and woman unclean (Lev 15:18).

- Touching a dead body, even being in the same room with a dead body, makes you unclean (Num 19).

To draw near to the sanctuary, Israelites have to be clean. Usually, they only have to wash their bodies and clothes and wait for the evening sacrifice. Sometimes, purification rites are more elaborate (cf. Lev 14; Num 19).

Because Yahweh is close, Israel also offers new forms of sacrifice. Like Cain, Abel, Noah, and Abraham, they still bring ascension offerings (Lev 1) and tribute offerings of grain (Lev 2). But new forms of sacrifice are introduced:

- Through the blood rites of the purification or sin offering (*hatt'at*), the priests cleanse the altars and the house from defilements of sin and uncleanness (Lev 4:1—5:13).
- Through the trespass offering (*'asham*), the priests compensate for aggressive, high-handed sins and for intrusions on holy things and holy space (Lev 5:14—6:7; 7:1-10).

If Israel's sins pollute Yahweh's house, He'll abandon it (Ezek 8-11). Israel offers these offerings to keep the sanctuary clean and to ensure that Yahweh sticks around. When Yahweh moves into Israel's neighborhood, He makes sure they have the tools they need to keep Him close by.

The other new offering is the peace offering (*shelem*). Like the purification and trespass offerings, the peace offering is never mentioned until Israel gets to Sinai (cf. Exod 20:24; 24:5). Unlike the purification and trespass offerings, the peace offering isn't for maintenance. It's a festive sacrifice that always culminates in a meal. It's the one offering an Israelite worshiper can eat.

In the Old Testament, the word "sacrifice" refers specifically to the peace offering. While Israel was in Egypt, Yahweh tells Pharaoh to let Israel go to "sacrifice" in the wilderness (Exod 3:18). He wants to bring Israel out of Egypt to *feed* them. That's the goal of the exodus: Yahweh bares His mighty arm so Israel can join Him for a party at the mountain.

The peace offering is a vision of a redeemed world. It depicts the world as it ought to be: God's people gathered with Him to enjoy the fruits of creation in His presence. In a world filled with tables of demons, the peace offering is an invitation to share in the table of the Lord. The peace offering, in short, is an Old Testament form of the Lord's Supper.

We can be more specific. There were three types of peace offering: Votive offerings fulfilled vows; free will offerings were expressions of praise; thanksgiving offerings (*todah*) showed gratitude for a specific blessing. The *todah* is the closest analogy to the Lord's Supper: It's a thanksgiving meal, accompanied by prayers and songs of thanks (Pss 69:30; 107:22; 116:17).

In introducing these new offerings, Yahweh also specifies ritual procedures. For the first time, we learn *how* to do an ascension offering, a tribute, a peace offering. There's a skeletal structure that runs across all the animal offerings:

1. The worshiper presents an animal and *leans his hand* on its head. By this gesture, the worshiper identifies with the animal and "ordains" it to represent him as it approaches Yahweh's presence.
2. The worshiper *slaughters* the animal. No one can pass the cherubim at Yahweh's gate without dying. The animal takes the curse of death as a substitute for the worshiper.
3. Slaughter isn't the end of the rite. After the worshiper kills the animal, the *priest sprinkles blood* on the altar. Blood purifies, turns away death, and opens doors.
4. Once the altar is smeared with blood, the priest dismembers the animal and places it in the *fire*. Yahweh lit the fire from His own fiery being (Lev 9:24; Deut 4:24). Entering the fire, the animal enters Yahweh's presence. More, the animal is changed into smoke and fire. This isn't

SACRIFICE

punishment. It's transfiguration, even deification, like Adam being glorified into Adam-and-Eve. This is the aim of the animal offerings: Through the animal, the worshiper unites with the God who is a consuming fire, whose love is an eternal flame.

5. All animal offerings are food rituals. At the end of a sacrifice, someone *eats*. Sometimes only Yahweh eats. Sometimes only the priests join Him. Sometimes the worshiper joins the priests to feast with Yahweh.

I've taught my kids and grandkids a chant to help them remember this:

> **Lay** the **hand**
> **Slay** the **beast**
> **Spread** the **blood**
> **Burn** the **flesh**
> **Eat** the **meal**.

You've got to do it rhythmically, accenting the bold-faced syllables, or it doesn't work. Preferably while stomping your feet.

This sacrificial sequence gives a skeletal order of service for Christian worship, the fulfilled sacrificial ritual:

1. We enter the presence of Yahweh only through our substitute, the Lord Jesus. We "lay hands" on Him as our priest.
2. God accepts us, but we still sins, and we should confess them. When the church gathers, she should confess her sins as a body. When we confess our sins, the Lord cleanses us from all unrighteousness (1 John 1:9–10). The minister declares we are forgiven.
3. We are dismembered by the Word, the sword of the Spirit that divides soul and spirit, joints and marrow (Heb 4:11–12).
4. By Word and Spirit, we're incorporated into the fiery presence of the Lord, transfigured into His image.
5. Having ascended to the throne, we're seated as kings at the Lord's royal table.

Each offering follows the same basic ritual but differs at a crucial point:

1. The "purification offering" (*hatt'at*) highlights the blood rite (Lev 4). In the other offerings, the priest dashes blood against the side of the altar. But the blood of the purification offering has to be smeared on the horns of the altar and poured at the base of the altar. Sometimes the blood is taken into the Holy Place and smeared on the horns of the golden altar.
2. The "ascension offering" (*'olah*) highlights the burning (Lev 1). The entire animal is burned. No human being eats any of the meat. It all belongs to Yahweh.
3. The "peace offering" (*shelem*) emphasizes the meal (Lev 3). Non-priests are only allowed to eat meat from the peace offering.

When you put these in order, you have this sequence: purification, ascension, meal. And this is precisely their order whenever they are performed at the same time (Lev 9:1–7; Num 6:13–20; 2 Chr 29:20–36). First the worshiper is purified, then he ascends, then he feasts in the Lord's presence. This is also the order of the original covenant-making ceremony at Mount Sinai (Exod 19–24). Israel cleanses themselves at the foot of Sinai. Then Moses ascends to receive the law. Finally, representatives of Israel eat and drink on the mountainside.

Translated into New Testamentese, purification, ascent, meal mean this: Confession and cleansing, ascent to receive the word, communion; mourning for sin, instruction in the way of life, thanksgiving and dismissal. That's the structure of biblical worship and the basic structure of nearly every Christian liturgy throughout history.

If our worship services don't look like that, we're not worshiping biblically. If we don't confess our sins at the beginning of the service, we shouldn't presume to go through the gate. If we don't get cut apart by the sword of the Word, we can't be put together again. If we don't end the service with a meal, what's the point of coming in the first place?

The Lord loves obedience and mercy more than sacrifice (1 Sam 15:22; Matt 9:13; 12:7, 33). When Israel offers sacrifices with blood-stained hands and sin-stained hearts, the Lord rejects them (Isa 1). The church can go through all the proper motions, conform to all the rubrics, say all the right words and do all the right gestures, and *still* offer a putrid stench instead of a soothing aroma. The *forms* of the liturgy are acceptable only if they conform to God's word. We *performers* of the liturgy are acceptable only if we walk in faith, obedience, compassion, love, humility, and justice.

God doesn't want the blood of bulls and goats. He delights in contrite hearts (Psa 51:17; Isa 57:15) and the sacrifice of the open ear (Psa 40:6-8), worshipers attentively obedient to His every word. He wants our liturgical sacrifice to express a sincere offering of our hearts, bodies, and lives.

Political Sacrifice

Viewing Christian worship from the perspective of Levitical sacrifice helps us see the depths of the liturgy and its cultural and political impact. We might think church is only a teaching time or an opportunity to get an emotional jolt from the music. In fact, we're doing in reality what ancient Israelites did in symbol. Adam's "sacrifice" in Eden is the first sacrifice, and it is a human sacrifice. Israel replicates that sacrifice figuratively, using animals. Jesus offers the first true sacrifice, a voluntary *human* sacrifice, by which He passes through death and ascends to the Father.

After Jesus, *because* of Jesus, sacrifice is humanized. It's humanized in the church. In the liturgy, we replicate Old Testa-

THEOPOLITAN LITURGY

ment figurative offerings in reality; our offerings are like Jesus' offering, real human self-sacrifices. It's blood, fire, and smoke, dismemberment and bodies rising from the dead. It's a meal where we eat the God-man so that He lives in us and we live in Him. We do in the open what Israel did under the shadows.

Sacrifice is also humanized politically and culturally. Liberal societies fool themselves into thinking we can do without sacrifice. The Roman Senate began with animal sacrifice, but not the U.S. Senate. No President or Prime Minister reads entrails; at least none admits to it.

Liberalism claims to order society without reference to God or gods. Politics is about human power and doesn't need to establish any sacrificial connection with the powers of the cosmos. Liberalism says we can have progress without catastrophe, that we can rise to glory without dying. Liberals believe in resurrection without a cross.

We think life can go on without death. To prove it, we shove death and the dying into closed clinical spaces where we don't have to see or think much about them. We resist self-sacrifice. Self-preservation is the highest good.

This is all a trick. Liberal societies still demand sacrifices. Not animal sacrifices, of course, but *human* ones. Modern liberal societies are Christianized enough to humanize sacrifice. They aren't Christianized enough to imitate Jesus' self-sacrifice. Instead, they demand sacrifices to human deities like the nation and the people or abstractions like Freedom and Democracy.

Totalitarian regimes are also modern sacrificial machines. They demand total sacrifice from their subjects, plant Killing Fields, and slaughter millions so that a "new man" can rise from the wreckage. They conquer and kill not just to extend territory but to fulfill their dream of a classless society, of Jew-free national socialism, of the utopia *du jour*.

The early church entered a world flush with sacrifice, and the modern church is no different. Wherever the church goes, she encounters a world organized by sacrifice, with its own idolatrous gestures, its own false atonements, its own empty promises of glory and life.

The church preaches the gospel and calls the nations into union with Jesus' self-sacrifice to the Father. She calls the nations to offer true sacrifice, a sacrifice of witness and praise like the sacrifice of Jesus.

She calls the nations into the realm of redeemed sacrifice, that is, into the liturgy. The church's liturgy re-orients the sacrificial habits of the world toward the true sacrifice of the kingdom. It puts sacrifice back in sync with the sacrificial patterns of God's creation. In the liturgy, sacrifice is being Christianized so that the sacrifices of the cities of men may be redeemed and reoriented toward the sacrifices of the heavenly city.

After Jesus, we have only a few choices. Sacrifice has been humanized, and societies will either cling to the sacrifice of Jesus enacted in the Eucharistic liturgy or will invent fresh forms of human slaughter and turn history into a charnel house. We face the choice between the peaceful sacrifice at the Lord's table or the violent sacrifices of secular order.

The Eucharist remakes the world because it redeems the perverse sacrifices of the world. Had Idi Amin, Stalin, or Pol Pot repented and taken a place at the Lord's table, their lives of brutal slaughter would have been redirected from their idolatries. Joined to the sacrifice of Jesus, their perverse sacrifices would have been corrected and, for the first time, they would have participated in a true human sacrifice.

Sacrifice of Praise

The liturgy redirects secular human sacrifice into the true human sacrifice of *praise*.

From Sinai to the end of the Old Testament, Israel's worship follows Torah. They offer animal and grain offerings at the Lord's house and keep the cycle of feasts laid out in Exodus, Leviticus, and Deuteronomy.

But there are dramatic changes along the way. As we saw in chapter 1, the tabernacle is ripped apart and never rebuilt. Instead, the Lord raises up Solomon to build a new sanctuary, the temple.

More importantly, Yahweh directs David to reorganize Israel's worship. He reorganizes the priesthood, dividing the descendants of Aaron into twenty-four clans, which serve two-week stints at the temple. The most interesting change has to do with music. David is the sweet Psalmist of Israel. He composes hymns and invents musical instruments. He also creates a musical culture in Israel. Before Solomon builds a temple of stone, David has orchestrated a living temple of song.

Priests blew silver trumpets at the tabernacle (Num 10) and at Jericho (Josh 6). Otherwise, they seem to be a quiet clan. Along come Israel's kings, and suddenly there's music everywhere. Saul knows he will become king when he meets a band of prophets singing and playing music, and he joins them (1 Sam 10:5–6). David sings and plays while he's on the run from Saul (Psa 18; 52; 54).[3]

Everywhere, kings make and inspire music. When a king takes his throne, his people sing and play music. Kings ascend to their thrones on the praises of the people, like the Lamb whose appearance in heaven sparks thunderous song (Rev 5). Music is a royal art. To sing, you must rule your body and breath. To make a musical instrument, you have to take dominion over a portion of creation and shape it into something beautiful that makes beautiful sounds.

---

[3] These paragraphs overlap with my discussion of Psalm-singing in *The Theopolitan Vision*, 44–46.

SACRIFICE

Music is a militant art. In preparation for the temple, David and the leaders of the army establish a permanent orchestra and choir (1 Chr 25:1). The military's involvement is noteworthy, a signal that temple music is part of Israel's arsenal. When the Moabites and the Ammonites attack Israel during Jehoshaphat's reign, he puts the special forces in front of the army—the Levitical choir, who sing destruction to their enemies (2 Chr 20). Martyrs go to the stake and the arena singing (Rev 14). Song equips worshipers psychologically, spiritually, and physically for Spiritual war. A church that sings together fights together. As the city of God sings, we offer true sacrifice in cities of false sacrifice.

Song is prophetic too. Singers "prophesy" (1 Chr 25:1) because the Spirit of prophecy inspires song (Eph 5:18-19). When martyrs sing, they glimpse their future vindication. When we sing of God's victory before it happens, we enter into that victory yet to come.

Priests are the main music-makers in Scripture. Once David becomes king, he brings the ark of the covenant to Jerusalem in a procession led by priestly musicians (1 Chr 15:16). After he installs the ark in its tent, he arranges for continuous musical worship (1 Chr 16), which is incorporated into the temple (1 Chr 25).

David doesn't just add a new dimension to Israel's worship. Something more profound is going on. A change of priesthood sparks a liturgical revolution. Sacrificial and priestly terminology is transferred to song. Music becomes a form of priestly service (1 Chr 15:2). As Levites once carried the furniture of the tabernacle, so now they "bear" the Lord in song (1 Chr 15:22, 26). Music becomes a form of priestly "work" (1 Chr 6:31-32; 23:25-32).

Priests guard the sanctuary. Music now takes over that function as a guardian of tradition (1 Chr 25:8). Singing Psalm 78 or the Song of Moses in Deuteronomy 32, Israel preserves her corporate memory and hands it over to a new generation.

Sacrifices are "memorials" before Yahweh (cf. Lev 2:2, 9, 16). A "memorial" reminds *God* of His promises so He will continue to keep them. Like the rainbow after the flood, a sacrifice calls on Yahweh to keep His word to Israel. In the temple liturgy, song becomes a form of memorial (1 Chr 16:4). As Israel sings of Yahweh's heroism, she calls Him to be the hero again and again.

It's hard to exaggerate the importance of David's innovations. It's a step toward the new covenant when we no longer slaughter and burn animals at all. Augustine said animal offerings were "figurative" offerings. The real sacrifice is always human self-sacrifice, pre-eminently that of Jesus. As he prepares for the temple worship, David introduces the true form of sacrifice, sacrifice fulfilled in song. We now offer sacrifices of song because the King has come.

The Spirit is the music of God and inspires song (Eph 5:18–19). We sing in and by the Spirit, and it would be a contradiction to sing in the Spirit while also grieving Him. Just as Yahweh hates Israel's offerings when they're mingled with oppression, so our songs may be drowned out by the cries of orphans and widows we abuse. The Father closes His ears to the songs of lying lips. He recoils when we have the smell of death on our breath (Psa 5:9).

Love Duet

David's liturgical innovations have some uncomfortable implications for worship. Think of how central sacrifice was to Israel's worship. Pretty central, right? Then think: Song is introduced to accompany animal offerings and then takes over the place of animal offerings. Then think: Perhaps *music* should be as central to Christian worship as sacrifice was to Israel's worship.

Few churches face up to this implication. A church that wouldn't think of hiring a pastor without a seminary degree will farm out the music to anyone who can read music or carry a tune. Churches that pay careful attention to the doctrinal content of the words often pay scant attention to the musical quality of the notes. Some churches ride the wave of tradition, singing golden oldies whether or not they're good oldies. Churches with contemporary worship get tossed to and fro by waves of fashion.

If song is our form of sacrifice, it deserves more attention, time, expertise, training. If song is our form of sacrifice, we should devote considerable effort to learn the songs of Scripture, the Psalms and other canticles that have been the primary songbook of the church for two thousand years.

Temple song has another important implication for worship. Sacrifice pervades Israel's worship. It's what Israel's worship *is*. *Christian* sacrifice should pervade Christian worship, and that means the service should be *sung*.

We saw in the last chapter that worship is a dialogue, a communion in speech between Jesus and His Bride. Spoken dialogue is good. A spoken liturgy sounds a little like boot camp, with the recruits standing straight and answering every bark from the commander with a firm "Hoo-Ha, Sergeant!" A sung liturgy is *better* because it captures the erotic dimension of the liturgy. Friends speak to one another. A drill sergeant shouts at his troops. Lovers *sing*. Jesus the Bridegroom calls a man to sing His love song to His Bride.

Are you a pastor who croaks through the hymns and keeps his voice down? There are options. Take the time and make the effort to learn to sing. Find a cantor to lead the church's singing. At least aspire to make the liturgy a fully sacrificial dialogue, that is, a dialogic sacrifice of *song*.

Eucharistic Sacrifice

We can't leave sacrifice without addressing one more topic more directly: The Lord's Supper. Is it, or is it not, a "sacrificial" meal? That's a question that divides the church. Catholics say,

"Yes." Protestants typically say, "No." Few ask what "sacrifice" means.

From the start of this chapter, we've seen sacrifice isn't only or mainly about killing and dismembering. Sacrifice is a ritual movement through death to new and better life. It's the progress of Adam to Adam-and-Eve, of Noah through the flood into a new creation, of Israel escaping Egypt through the death-waters of the Red Sea. It's the passage of Jesus through cross and grave to His Father's right hand.

If the question is, "Is Jesus crucified all over again at the Supper?" the answer is clear: No, of course not, and few, if any, teachers in the church have ever taught anything that crude. If the question is, "Do we pass through death into new life in union with Jesus at the Supper?" the answer is "Yes."

The Eucharist is a "memorial" of Jesus' death, a "reminder" to the Father of His self-offering. The Eucharist is a sacrifice of praise. But it's more: It renews our union with Jesus' death and resurrection, a union forged in baptism (Rom 6:1–14). As we participate every week in the Eucharist, we pass again and again from death into new life. As we eat and drink Christ's body and blood, we're conformed to his sacrifice, so our entire life becomes "reasonable service," a liturgy of self-offering in which we, like Jesus, are priests of our own self-sacrifice. As we share this sacrificial meal, we're made over into martyrs, willing to shed our life's blood in faithful witness.

4 TIME

Then God said, "Let there be lights in the expanse of the heavens to separate the day from the night, and let them be for signs and for seasons and for days and years;
Genesis 1:14

The creation account reads like the rubrics of a prayer book. Day after day, God runs through the same series of actions:

> God speaks.
> God names.
> God sees and pronounces it good.

During the first three days, God divides. On Day 1, it's:

> God speaks light.
> God sees the light is good.
> God divides day and night, and sets them in a sequence.
> God names light "day," and darkness "night."

Then Day 2:

> God speaks a firmament.
> The firmament separates waters above and below.
> God calls the firmament heaven.

Then Day 3:

> God speaks in order to separate waters and land.
> God names the dry land "earth," the waters "sea."
> God sees and pronounces it good.

After that, God starts filling the heaven, seas, and earth. He calls plants to sprout on earth, speaks the sun, moon and stars into the firmament, summons the waters to teem with swimming things and the earth and heaven to be filled with birds, makes land animals, creepers, and man from the ground.

Over and over, God repeats the same series of actions: speaking, making, seeing, judging; speaking, dividing, naming, pronouncing. Each day is a variation on the theme. The days aren't identical, but they're repetitive.

The creation week gives us a shadowy glimpse of the Trinity as God (*'elohim*) speaks His Word while His Spirit hovers. God speaks to start a day, and God speaks back to Himself to end each day. Creation comes to be through a divine liturgy as God, the Spirit, and the Word speak and speak back, call and respond. Creation emerges from the trialogue of Father, Word, and Spirit.

By the end of the week, God has created a full world of space and time. True, Genesis 1 doesn't use the word "time." It uses words like "light" and "darkness," "day" and "night," "evening" and "morning." Without using the word "time," Genesis 1 describes what we mean when we say "time." God's rhythmic work of creation sets creation's temporal rhythms ticking and tocking.

God establishes the rhythm of the day on Day 1, and every day follows the pattern. Evening and morning, Day 1. Evening and morning, Day 2. Evening and morning, Day 3. You get the point. It keeps going until it's "Evening and morning, *yesterday*." Like God's own creative work, the world moves in a pattern of non-identical repetition.

God creates liturgically. His actions are liturgical. And creation dances a liturgical dance of evenings and mornings, light and dark.

Scholars sometimes talk about "liturgical time" as if it's a species of time imposed on the "natural time" measured by the motion of the sun, moon, and stars. The Bible doesn't present things that way. The motion of sun, moon, and stars is *itself* a liturgical motion, a heavenly liturgy.

"Liturgical time" isn't a spiritual or religious layer on top of "real time" or "scientific time" or "clock time." Time *is* liturgical, created in liturgy and choreographed by the divine Liturgist. It's liturgy all the way down.

Appointed Times

I'm not speculating or playing with words. The Bible actually uses liturgical language to describe creation's temporal movements.

Initially, God oversees creation's time directly (Gen 1:3–5). For three days, light follows darkness, and darkness follows light. But the light doesn't come from sunrise, and the darkness doesn't follow sunset. There's a simple reason for that: There's no sun. Wherever the light comes from, *God* is orchestrating it.

Then on Day 4, He makes created lights—the greater light of day, the lesser light of night, and the stars (Gen 1:14–19). He's been keeping time Himself, but after Day 4, He gives *creatures* authority over time. For three days, the Creator is Lord of time all by Himself. After Day 4, He *delegates* the rule of time. Sun, moon, and stars become the first created time lords.

Sun, moon, and stars have critical physical, biological, and cultural functions in the universe. All life on earth depends on the sun. The moon drags the tides to and from the sandy shore. Stars help sailors navigate the wine-dark seas.

Those *aren't* the purposes mentioned in Genesis 1. Heavenly lights "separate" day and night (Gen 1:14). That's what *Yahweh* has been doing in the first part of the creation week (Gen 1:4, 6). Now He empowers created things to take up this divine task. Heavenly lights also "govern" the day and night (1:16). Again, God delegates authority to creatures to rule creation, to participate in creation's own fulfillment. Even before man and woman were placed on the earth, the earth had creaturely rulers.

Sun, moon, and stars are also created "for signs, seasons, days and years" (Gen 1:14). "Days and years" is pretty straightforward. We know the day is over when the sun sets. We track months by phases of the moon. When the sun returns to springtime position in relation to the Zodiac, a year has passed.

"Signs" are less obvious. Astrologists today look to the heavens to suss out the future, but sane people know that's bogus. Still, God creates the heavens to communicate. In the Bible, people *do* see signs in the heavens, and the heavens do speak. Even if we can't predict the future by looking at stars, the heavenly lights signify: "The heavens are telling of the glory of God, and the firmament is declaring the work of His hands" (Psa 19:1).

For my purposes, the most important term is "seasons" (Heb. *mo'ed*). The Hebrew word doesn't refer to the cycle of winter, spring, summer, fall. It means "appointed times" and usually refers to the times of Israel's festivals (Exod 13:10; 23:15).

How do ancient Israelites know when to celebrate Passover? Passover happens on the night of the first full moon after the beginning of spring, the vernal equinox. The month of Passover is the first month of Israel's liturgical year (Exod 12:2), and other feasts are dated by counting from Passover. Israelites know appointed times because they look at the night sky. The heavens are tracking "seasons."

Israel doesn't read this liturgical meaning *into* the sky. They don't make it up. God *creates* the sky as a liturgical calendar. Sun, moon, and stars exist to indicate the appointed times. Created time is liturgical, and Israel's time ticks and tocks along with the movements of the universe.

The phrase "*appointed* time" is important. Think of an "appointment" for a meeting or, even better, a "date." Yahweh sets times when He promises to meet with Israel, marked by heavenly lights. He sets dates with His Bride, when she visits His house to commune with Him. *Mo'ed* is the word for "meeting" in the phrase "tent of meeting" (Exod 27:21; 28:43; 29:4, 10; etc.). God's tent is the place where He keeps appointments, where Israel gathers at the appointed times. Creation is designed to make sure Israel's timing is right, to keep them from showing up in an untimely way.

We'll look at Israel's cycle of feasts below and think about how it's transformed into the Christian calendar. For now, just notice this: Creation is organized liturgically. The sun, the vast galaxies of stars, the light of the silvery moon, are set up to show the Bride when she can be with her Beloved.

Sabbath

There's another hint that created time is liturgical time: Day 7, the Sabbath. Yahweh completes His work, rests, blesses and sanctifies the day (Gen 2:1–3). Exodus later calls this day the "Sabbath," a pun on the Hebrew word for "seven" that means "ceasing" (Exod 20:8–11).

The Sabbath isn't just a day of "ceasing." It's a day for celebration. Yahweh completes His work. He's said all the week that creation is good. At the end, He says it's "very good" (Gen 1:31). A job well done, and Yahweh takes time to delight in it. He enters into His joy.

Sabbath is also a day of enthronement. As we saw in chapter 1, the tabernacle is a small replica of creation.

After Moses "completes" the work of building the tabernacle, Yahweh descends from Sinai to take His throne above the cherubim in the Most Holy Place (Exod 40:34–38). After Solomon "completes" the microcosmic temple, Yahweh fills the house with His glory (1 Kgs 8:10–11). Sabbath is for ceasing. Sabbath is also a day of royal splendor.

Each day of the creation week includes a mini-Sabbath. Yahweh establishes the pattern of day and night and then works within that pattern. He does something new each day and ceases each night. Like the week, each day is divided into work-time and rest-time, time for labor and time for joy. Each day has a Sabbatical, liturgical structure.

The Sabbath connects the liturgy of God's cosmic time with human time-keeping. There's nothing in the earth or sky to indicate that our time should be organized in units of 6 + 1. But it's not arbitrary. We observe weeks as well as days, months, and years because God sets the pattern in the creation week. God's days are rhythmical, and His weeks are rhythmical. So are ours.

Some theologians think men and women start keeping Sabbath as soon as they're created. From Adam, they say, human beings work six days and rest on the seventh, following Yahweh's example. We don't know for sure whether or not early humans ceased from their labor on the seventh day. They *may* have, but the Bible never tells us. I suspect they didn't. Adam is supposed to join Yahweh in enthroned rest as prince of creation. Because of his sin, like Israel later, he doesn't enter into rest (Psa 95; Heb 4).

Noah's name means "rest." He "brings rest" to the world (Gen 5:29). We're not told that he keeps Sabbath, but we *do* know he becomes a king after the flood. He's given authority to execute murderers, and he enjoys the wine from the vineyard he plants. Wine is a Sabbatical, royal drink. Noah the rest-bringer becomes Noah the king. Sabbath probably isn't a creation ordinance. It's more likely a postdiluvian institution.

But the first *explicit* reference to human Sabbath-keeping doesn't occur until after the exodus. Pharaoh imposes an oppressive uniform time on Israel, an identical repetition of work-work-work, work-without-rest. After the exodus, Israel still has to work for their food, but not much. Yahweh provides miraculous food, manna from heaven and water from the rock. They don't have to plant, tend, and harvest. They gather. That's it. Yahweh opens His hand to satisfy their souls' desires.

That minimal work is ordered by God's pattern in the creation week. Yahweh forbids Israel to gather on the seventh day (Exod 16:22–26) and promises to provide seven days' worth of manna in six days. For the first time, human beings dance their weeks alongside Yahweh.

Israel's Sabbath-keeping is a continual reminder of her deliverance from Pharaoh. It's an *effective* sign of that deliverance, a sign that does what it signifies. So long as Israel keeps Sabbath, Israel's time is *actually* different from Egypt's time. Yahweh delivers Israel from Pharaoh's anti-liturgy of restless labor to enter His liturgical rhythm. This is what the exodus is for: to reorder Israel's time-keeping so it conforms to the Creator's. It's what salvation *is*: entry into a new time.

Keeping Sabbath is an act of faith, a confession of Israel's utter dependence on Yahweh. They have to trust Yahweh to provide two days' worth of manna on the sixth day. Some don't trust him and go searching for manna on the seventh day (Exod 16:27–30). Even after they enter the land, they keep Sabbath because they're still utterly dependent on His blessing to enjoy the fruits of the earth.

Sabbath is also a sign of Israel's glorification. They aren't just *freed* in the exodus. They're *exalted*, elevated to become Yahweh's treasured possession, His royal priesthood (Exod 19:5–6). They begin to share Yahweh's Sabbath enthronement as they share Yahweh's rest.

Every Sabbath after the exodus, Israel gathers for a "holy convocation" (Lev 23:3), enthroned again with Yahweh their Master. Ancient Israelites don't spend every Sabbath at the tabernacle or temple. That would be impossible. Danites living in the far north of Israel would spend half the week traveling to Jerusalem and the other half returning, just in time to head back to the temple. They wouldn't do any work to rest *from*. No, Israel has holy convocations every Sabbath, but they don't happen in one location. Levites are scattered in cities throughout the land, and there are Levitical and priestly cities. Every Sabbath, Israelites assemble in "synagogues" all over the land to praise Yahweh, learn Torah, and pray.

Most ancient peoples don't follow this rhythm. They have their own calendars, their own patterns of time-keeping. They keep appointed times with their idols. Like the Egyptians, they work without rest, or at least force their slaves to work without rest. Their holidays don't celebrate the mighty acts of Yahweh, the living God. Idolatrous time-keeping facilitates false worship and becomes an instrument of abuse. Throughout the ancient world, time is out of joint.

Except in Israel. By conforming to Yahweh's weekly routine, Israel keeps time with the time of creation. Israel's liturgical time becomes an echo of creation's original time. They're put in sync with the time of the cosmos. By celebrating God's mighty act in the Exodus, Israel's time keeps time with the time of redemption. Israel's liturgical calendar is the redemption of time.

We find again the same pattern we've seen in earlier chapters when examining place, language, and sacrifice. God creates a liturgical world, and man lives, moves, and has his being in the liturgical grooves cut by creation. After Adam's sin, cultures take on distorted shapes, which are put back in shape when God delivers sinners and incorporates them into His liturgical community. As it's done in obedience to God's Word, liturgy redeems time as, over years and centuries, it smooths the crooked time of the nations into a created image of the Creator's time-keeping.

Eighth Day

Most Christians don't worship on Saturday, at the end of the week. Jesus rises from the dead on the day *after* the Sabbath, on the first day of a new week. In a sense, it's a return to the origin. Adam is created on the sixth day, so his first full day of life is the seventh day, Yahweh's Sabbath. Jesus is the new Adam, restoring time's original balance. Jesus restores the priority of rest.

But Jesus doesn't restore the old. He doesn't turn the clock back to the beginning. Jesus' resurrection happens on the "eighth day" (John 20:26; cf. Exod 22:30; Lev 12:3), a day that bursts out of the calendrical constraints of the old creation. Jesus' resurrection inaugurates a new calendar.

The Lord's Day isn't identical to the Sabbath, but it is the designated day of worship. On this day, heaven and earth join. On this day, the Lord invites us into His house, calls us to join Him at the peak of heavenly Zion. On this day, He speaks to us and feeds us. The Lord's Day isn't just another day. It belongs to the Lord as His day of enthronement and judgment, which has become our day of enthronement.

Every time we assemble for worship, we declare a new Adam has arrived, bringing a new time and a new creation. We don't just *say* it's true. It *is* true as we assemble in the Spirit on the day of Jesus. Our worship is an entry into the new creation. We taste the final day already now, experiencing the new creation in the midst of the old.

Worshiping on the eighth day, we don't merely work in order to reach a day of rest. We do that. But the church's week goes the other way: We *start* the week in rest. We begin our work from a position of enthroned victory.

The peace, rest, and glory of the first day infuses the whole week. As Karl Barth said, a man who prays on Sunday will pray throughout the week. A man who gives thanks on Sunday will live a life of gratitude. A man who rejoices in the Lord on the Lord's day will see every day as a day of the Lord, a day of joy. Each Lord's day, we taste the last day, and the taste lingers through and spices up our work days.

On the Sabbath, Israel already shares in Yahweh's enthronement. But they don't share fully. No one, not even the high priest, goes into Yahweh's throne room—the Most Holy Place—and climbs up to sit above the cherubim. Our Priest has done just that because Jesus the Priest is also Jesus the King. He offers Himself once for all, rips the curtain of the temple, and processes upwards in glory to share His Father's throne.

He doesn't do it alone. Jesus has taken our flesh to make a way *for us*. He's above all rule and authority, enthroned in heavenly places. Because we're in Him as His body, so are wewe're in the heavenlies too (Eph 1:21–23; 2:6). He makes us kings and priests and shares His throne, which is His *Father's* throne, with us, His Bride (Rev 3:21). The Lord's day isn't a "break" from the turmoil of daily life. On the Lord's day, the Lord sifts and judges us, declares His royal word, gives us our marching orders. On the Lord's day, *we* sit on thrones to declare, judge, rule. Nothing affects the world so much as what the church says and does in our prayers, praises, and proclamation on the Lord's day.

Remember what I said about the sun, moon, and stars a few pages ago? God delegates authority to the heavenly lights to govern time. But they don't keep governing time. God gives *man* that authority.

It starts happening already in the Old Testament. In Genesis 14:1, we read about the "thirteenth year of Chedorlaomer." Huh, how'd *he* get his name on a year? Throughout Israel's

TIME

monarchy, time is named by the names and numbers of kings. As Israel slides toward exile, we enter the "times of the Gentiles," when Gentile emperors imprint their names to time periods (e.g., the "days of Nebuchadnezzar"). You see what's going on? At first, sun, moon and stars "rule" time. Once kings come into the picture, they take over. They govern time because they're like lights in the heavens and stars in the firmament.

That's all preparation for the new era that comes with Jesus. Jesus comes in the fullness of time. As God-Man, He is Lord of ages, who has inscribed His name on our calendars (this is A.D. 2019) He graciously shares His status with us. *We're* in the heavens, shining like stars (Phil 2:15). We are sons, exalted with Jesus above the angels (Heb 1:1–13). Once heavenly lights ruled time. *We* are the new time lords.

"We" here means "we Christians" or "we members of Christ's body." Jesus separates the times. But we're with Jesus, and so this is *our* time too. We can abuse this authority, lording it over time as if we were autonomous. We can make a relentless 24/7 news cycle, an Egyptian system of work without rest. All human lordship must submit to the decrees of the High Lord. But that potential for abuse doesn't change the reality: We're the heavenly clocks of the new covenant.

Christians used to know this. Christopher Page has described medieval Christendom as a "soundscape." A medieval traveler knew he was back in the Christian world when he stopped hearing muezzins calling the hours of prayer and started hearing the chiming of bells. Bells clanged out liturgical hours with their giant iron tongues. They called the faithful to the Mass every Lord's day. In Christian Europe, liturgical time became the governing time for a whole civilization.

If we're the time lords, we don't determine when to celebrate feasts by looking at the phases of the moon. Paul goes apoplectic when Christians submit to the "elementary things" in the heavens

(Gal 4:8–11; Col 2:16). As time lords, we have authority to decide when and how to celebrate. We must organize time obediently. We can organize time well only if we have the tunes of creation and redemption running in an endless loop through the ears of our soul. But we've grown up, and God has given us the authority to shape time.

Israel's Calendar

The creation week establishes a weekly rhythm of work and rest, labor and liturgy. Yahweh sets the liturgy of time and later invites Israel and us to dance along.

The week isn't the only pattern of liturgical time built into the creation. As we've seen, the Lord creates the sun, moon, and stars to mark years, months, and appointed times as well as to govern day and night. God creates a world that sways to *multiple* rhythms.

Virtually no culture marks only days and weeks. Every thirty days or so, we start a new month. When we have passed through twelve moon-cycles, we say we've grown a year older. Day-night, day-night; week after week after week; month follows month follows month; and years crawl and then sprint by.

When God lays out Israel's liturgical calendar, it matches that complex created rhythm. He invites them to share His Sabbath every week. But He also instructs them to mark the beginning of each month (Num 28:11–15) and to punctuate years with an annual cycle of feasts (Exod 23:14–17; Lev 23; Deut 16).

On the first day of every month, the priests offer extra offerings at the sanctuary. They offer two male lambs every day and two more every Sabbath. At the beginning of each month, they offer even more—two bulls, a ram, and seven lambs (Num 28:11–15).

Three times a year, there are bigger festivals. At the beginning of the liturgical year, in spring, all Israelite men are required to appear before Yahweh to celebrate Passover and the week-long Feast of Unleavened Bread. From Passover, they count seven weeks, and when they get to fifty days, they keep Pentecost, also called the Feast of Weeks. That takes place in the third month of the liturgical year.

The seventh month is the final month of the liturgical calendar, and it's jammed with festivity. The month begins with a special new moon feast called the Feast of Trumpets (Lev 23:23–25). On the tenth day, Israel fasts while the high priest performs the rites of the Day of Atonement, to purify the sanctuary and re-start the priesthood (Lev 16; 23:26–32). From the fifteenth to the twenty-second day, Israel celebrates the Feast of Booths, also known as the "Feast of Ingathering" (Lev 23:33–44).

We could spend a lot of time studying these feasts, but I'll confine myself to a few general points. Israel's feasts follow the natural cycle of the agricultural year. Passover and Unleavened Bread take place at spring planting, Pentecost is a "first fruits" festival, and Booths is a harvest feast. By observing these feasts, Israel acknowledges Yahweh as the Lord and Giver of life. He makes the earth fruitful.

The feasts also mark key events in Israel's history. Passover, of course, commemorates Israel's liberation from Egypt (Exod 12–13). Pentecost celebrates Israel's arrival at Sinai, the cutting of the covenant, and the giving of the law. Israel lives in "booths" during the Feast of Booths to remind them of their forty-year campout in the wilderness (Lev 23:42–43).

Every year, Israel lives through the founding events of her history all over again. It's a great teaching tool. Going through the rituals of Passover, Israelite children ask what it's all about, and their parents have a chance to retell the story of the exodus (Exod 12:25–27). They don't just tell the story but *re-enact* it.

It's more than a teaching tool. The feasts are "memorials" (Exod 12:14), like the offerings on the altar and the rainbow in the cloud. Feasts "remind" Yahweh of His promises. As they commemorate Passover, Israel asks Yahweh to liberate them from other enemies—Midian, Philistia, Babylon. As they keep the feast of Pentecost, they call on Yahweh to keep the Sinai covenant.

The festival cycle also points ahead to Israel's future and the world's. As a harvest feast, the Feast of Booths expresses Israel's hope that the Lord will gather the nations into His house. It's hope performed as liturgy. During the week of the Feast of Booths, the priests offer a total of seventy bulls on the altar (Num 29:12–38). Seventy is the number of nations (Gen 10). The Feast of Booths anticipates the time when Gentiles will offer themselves as living sacrifices to the God of Israel.

The natural and historical dimensions of the feasts overlap and interpenetrate. Passover is the beginning, a "planting" of Israel among the nations. Pentecost is "first fruits," Israel the covenant people as the first harvest of nations. Booths represents the full harvest, not only of Israel but of the Gentiles.

Once again, we see "liturgical time" isn't alien to "real time." Time is inherently liturgical, and the specific liturgical calendar of Israel tracks with and enhances created liturgical cycles. The liturgical calendar is a calendar of *new* creation.

Early in Israel's history, Yahweh Himself lays out Israel's annual schedule of feasts. Later Israel's leaders *add* festivals to the calendar. After the Lord delivers Israel from Haman's plot, Mordecai establishes the annual festival of Purim (from Hebrew *pur*, meaning "lot") to commemorate this great deliverance (Est 9:20–32). During the "intertestamental" period, the Maccabees defeat the Syrian king Antiochus Epiphanes and recover Jerusalem. They institute the Feast of Dedication, known as Hanukkah, to celebrate the victory. Jesus celebrates the feast (John 10:22), so He must have thought it legitimate.

Given what we've seen, this isn't a surprise. Israel's leaders have the authority to organize the calendar. After all, they're on their way to becoming lords of time.

In its annual calendar, Israel stands in contrast to the nations. Her year is Yahwehized, fashioned both by created rhythms and by Yahweh's just and merciful works. Not so the Gentiles. Their annual calendars celebrate the great moments of their own history, including festivals to their false gods. Their calendars take no notice of their Creator or His works. In a world of broken time, Israel alone keeps time faithfully.

But Israel doesn't exist merely to stand in contrast. Israel calls the nations to worship Yahweh. As that happens, Gentiles reorder their time, adding celebrations of God's acts to their own time-keeping. As they conform to Israel's liturgical time, their time begins to be redeemed, reoriented toward God's past works and His future harvest of nations. They begin to redeem the times.

The Church's Year

For most of her history, the church has followed Israel's example in keeping an annual as well as a weekly liturgical cycle. Like Israel's calendar, the church calendar marks specific events of redemptive history: Christmas celebrates the birth of Jesus, Good Friday commemorates the cross, Easter celebrates the resurrection, and Pentecost gives thanks for the gift of the Spirit.

The New Testament doesn't mention any of these Christian feasts, and some Christians think it's wrong for the church to observe any feast besides the weekly Lord's Day. Since it's not commanded, it's forbidden. But we aren't children any more. Our calendar isn't controlled by the sun, moon, and stars. We don't need direct revelation from God to schedule times with the Bridegroom. We're in heavenly places with Jesus as time lords.

The church's leaders, like Mordecai, have authority to establish feasts and commemorations in keeping with the model of Israel's calendar, which is laid out so carefully in the Bible.

So the church has arranged the whole year around the life of Jesus. The Western church's calendar begins late in the calendar year with Advent ("Coming" or "Arrival"), a four-week season of preparation before Christmas. During Advent, the church meditates on the many ways the Lord comes. We remember Israel's longing for the advent of the Messiah and renew our longing for His final advent.

Christmas, of course, celebrates the human birth of the Son of God. It's followed by several weeks of "Epiphany" ("Manifestation"), which focus on events that radiate Jesus' Messianic vocation and power—His baptism, the wedding at Cana, His miracles and healings, the Transfiguration.

After Epiphany comes Lent, a forty-day period of fasting devoted to meditation on the suffering and death of Jesus. Lent climaxes in Holy Week, which walks through the final week of Jesus' life, His Last Supper (on Maundy Thursday), and His trials and death (on Good Friday).

Some churches observe Holy Saturday, the day when Jesus lies dead in the tomb. After the fast of Lent and Holy Week comes the glory of Easter. Easter isn't a single day but lasts through the whole of the forty-day period until Ascension. It takes weeks to grasp the joy of resurrection.

Ascension Day has been under-celebrated throughout the history of the church. Most churches recognize it, but it doesn't get the emphasis it deserves. As Jesus tells Pilate, He's born for the purpose of becoming a king. The gospel is the announcement that Jesus is the Davidic king (Rom 1:1–4). Ascension is the climax of the gospel narrative and should be celebrated as such.

After Jesus ascends, He gives His coronation gift to His Bride. That gift is the Spirit, who unites the church with Christ, animates the body, gives gifts to the members so each can serve and edify the whole.

The Sunday after Pentecost is "Trinity Sunday." The whole of the church calendar unveils the Trinity. The Father sends the Son at Advent and Christmas, and the Son manifests the glory of the Father during Epiphany. He offers Himself as a perfect sacrifice to the Father on Good Friday, and the Father rewards His self-offering by raising Him from the dead. Ascended to His Father, he receives the Spirit, whom He pours out on the disciples.

Jesus comes from the Father to reveal the Father and then returns to the Father. Jesus receives and gives the Spirit, who unites us to Jesus so we can go to the Father. Father to Son to Spirit, who catches us up in the Son's movement to the Father.

As we observe the church year, we are brought into this Triune movement. The rhythms of historical time are incorporated into the rhythms of Father, Son, and Spirit. In the liturgical calendar, our time is taken up into the life of the Trinity.

Daily Office

Many churches have danced another liturgical dance, the tiny dance of the day. In the early centuries, some churches gathered several times a day for public prayers. Days began with Matins and ended with Vespers. With the rise of monasticism, the daily cycle of prayers disappeared into the cloistered confines of the monastery. Instead of morning and evening prayers, monks kept a twenty-four-hour cycle that included eight times of prayers. No one with a day job could keep up. Monks prayed on behalf of everyone else.

Some Protestant churches attempted to revive the daily office for lay Christians. In the *Book of Common Prayer*, there are services for Matins and Evensong (Vespers), and these services are observed in Anglican churches around the world. Sadly, the daily office has largely disappeared from the church.

It should be revived. The daily office has biblical roots. At the tabernacle and temple, priests begin each day by offering an ascension offering, establishing a communion of prayer between heaven and earth. They end each day with an evening offering (Num 28:1-8). The offerings cohere with the temporal rhythm of the creation week, with its evenings and mornings. Each day becomes a day of new creation, a new stage in the Creator's work of forming and filling.

Under the law, these daily offerings affect everyone in the entire land, including those far from the central sanctuary. An Israelite who becomes unclean has to wash himself and wait till evening to become clean (e.g., Lev 15:5-11). Why wait till evening? Because his impurity is removed by the evening offering. By "baptizing" himself, he participates in the cleansing effect of the offering.

As long as the temple stands, the apostles observe these hours of prayer. Peter and John heal a man as they come to the temple at the ninth hour for prayer (Acts 3:1).

Christians today have a daily habit of prayer. They pray, read Scripture, or meditate privately or with their families every morning and evening. That's good. But it's better for a church to *gather* daily, morning and evening. It's better for worship to be public. It's better for daily time, as well as weekly and annual time, to be organized liturgically.

Few may show up to daily offerings of prayer. It doesn't matter. Jesus promises to be present where two or three are gathered. And if Jesus is there, the church has all she needs to commune in dialogue with her Lord. Her prayers, like the offerings of Israel, spread out to affect the world around her. Her prayers aren't just for her but for "all sorts and conditions of men," for rulers and nations. Her public daily prayers have public effects.

Following the example of Israel, following the apostolic

TIME

precedent, we keep a liturgical calendar, including daily offices, to ensure that time is thoroughly Christianized, from top to bottom, from the year down to the day.

Time Turned Christian

I can hear the objections. Isn't this esoteric and irrelevant? What difference does the church calendar make? Shouldn't we be thinking about more important things? If we want the gospel to change the world, shouldn't we focus on mission?

Such objections are superficial. Few things are more important to a culture than its time-keeping, and there can be no more fundamental cultural change than a change of time. The Christian calendar *is* a missional issue. It's all about transforming the city of man into an image of the future city of God.

History takes its place on the calendar before, and more permanently, than in the textbooks. Change the calendar, and you change the way time is experienced and organized. Change the calendar, and you change the rhythm of life. Add Martin Luther King Day, and you've embedded the Civil Rights movement in American government, public education, entertainment. Turn "Christmas" into "Winter Holiday," and you've de-Christianized one part of the year. Think of the epochal change when the Roman world acknowledged that Jesus, an obscure Jew, was the crux of the ages. Think of what it would mean for China to adopt a Christian calendar: A billion people and more would enter the Christian era.

The gospel alters and redeems time. God enters time so that through time, He saves and glorifies the world. Because of Jesus' death and resurrection, time isn't progress toward death. Death is swallowed up by life. Time moves toward resurrection.

That change of times lies at the heart of our calendars, in the distinction between "Before Christ" and "Anno Domini,"

"In the Year of our Lord." B.C. counts down, like a bomb about to detonate. A.D. moves upward toward eternity.

Every revolutionary movement in the modern world has attempted to start time over again. French Revolutionaries tried to renumber from 1789 as Year 1. Russian Revolutionaries rebooted time in 1918. They tried to turn the time of Jesus into a parenthesis. Jesus won. As I write this paragraph, France and Russia date their letters and laws with *A.D.* 2019, along with much of the rest of the world.

These movements were obviously heretical, implicitly denying Jesus is Lord of time. But this denial takes more subtle forms. Virtually every culture follows some annual calendrical pattern. In the United States, the Fourth of July, Independence Day, celebrates the sacred nation. In France, it's Bastille Day. In England, Guy Fawkes Day is about England's deliverance from Spain and the Papacy.

Days of remembrance are central to national identity. When we celebrate national holidays, we renew our commitment to the nation and its ideals. Holidays move us emotionally. It's hard for an American to watch fireworks and listen to the National Anthem without getting a lump in his throat.

Love for country is good. But the nation can displace the church in our order of affections and commitments. If we're to hate our father and mother to follow Jesus, we surely must be prepared to hate fatherland and mother country. The church is the Christian's primary community. Christians are citizens of *that* nation, residents of the *heavenly* city. While we're also citizens of other cities and other nations, the church claims our primary loyalty and love because it is the body of our Lord Jesus. Baptismal water is thicker than blood, and the church, born of water and the Spirit, is bound as one body more firmly, more substantially, than any nation born of fire and blood.

That means the church calendar must be the Christian's

primary calendar. When the church molds her time-keeping to the world's time-keeping, she becomes worldly at a fundamental level. The temporal rhythm of her life becomes worldly. The church calendar is a political and cultural and missional issue, a test of the faithfulness of the heavenly *polis* against its earthly challengers.

Because the church is an outpost of the heavenly city on earth, she must mark time differently. Her holidays must mark the great events of her history, which are the great events of world history. If we don't observe a liturgical calendar, we leave the twisted times of the nations in place. If we don't have a liturgical calendar, time isn't shaped by the life, death and resurrection of Jesus. If we refuse a church calendar, time isn't recognized as the time of Father, Son, and Spirit. In short, if liturgical time doesn't redeem time, time is unredeemed. If we let the world make the calendar, we're denying that Jesus matters. We're denying that He's Lord of time.

The liturgical calendar corrects the disjointed time-keeping of the world. The liturgical calendar is time-keeping conformed to God's work and will. When the church keeps the rhythm of redemptive history, redemption is inscribed on the temporal foundation of life. A church that keeps the liturgical calendar begins to Christianize time, keeping time in tune with the time of creation that will be fulfilled in the endless day of new creation.

5 JOY

*When the morning stars sang together And all
the sons of God shouted for joy*
Job 38:7

Remember how I described liturgy at the beginning of the book? Slow, repetitive, boring, boring, boring. Dead. And deadening.

That's how many Christians experience liturgy. Churches are often at fault. Some liturgies *are* deadening because they teach you to treat yourself like dirt. You grovel when you come in. You grovel during confession. The sermon is designed to make you grovel some more. You crawl to the communion rail to choke down a wafer and a sip of wine. Then you're sent out to invite other people to come grovel along with you. You might stand and sit, but you feel as if you spend the whole service on our knees, if not flat on your face.

Don't get me wrong. There's a place for abject confession and repentance. There are moments for kneeling and prostration. Every service should include a confession of sin, when it's best to kneel. But you don't come to church to stay on your knees. You lower yourself before the Lord so He can exalt you.

You're kings in the King. It's the Lord's day, the new covenant day of enthronement. The liturgy should be fit for kings.

It's the Lord's day, the fulfillment of Israel's Sabbath. On this day, we enter the Lord's own Sabbath, which is a day of joy and satisfaction. Yahweh ceases because He's finished. Ceasing, He enjoys the delights of what He's made.

In an important sense, our rest isn't like that. We're *never* finished. No matter how hard you work during the week, you never get *everything* done that needs doing. No matter how long you live, you'll leave unfinished projects scattered around your workroom or desk.

Yet the Lord invites us to rest anyway. Long before we're finished, the Lord tells us to rejoice *as if* we're finished. There's a promise in that: By instructing us to cease from work, He promises He'll give us time to complete the tasks He assigns to us. He promises us all the time we need.

We should take a liturgical lesson from all this. On His first Sabbath, Yahweh entered into satisfied delight in His work. For us, the Lord's day is a day of joy, a day to take delight in God's work for us. If we imitate the Lord's own Sabbath, it should also be a day for delight in our own work.

Some Christians are reluctant to discuss their work on the Lord's day. They fear they might contaminate the holy day with profane conversation. That's exactly wrong. The Lord's day isn't a sacred island in a secular world. It's a taste of the future in the midst of the present. On the Lord's day, we touch the day when our work comes to fruition in a new heavens and new earth. By talking about work, we're linking our labor with the great cosmic movement of history, from the first to the final temple.

The Lord's day gives a taste of new creation because it's a Eucharistic day. On the Lord's day, we eat bread and drink wine, products of human skill and work. Grain and fruit plants are the first products of earth (Gen 1:11). Eucharistic bread and wine are glorified grain and fruit, the first products of *new* creation. As a Eucharistic day, the Lord's day is a day of joy, gladness not glumness, delightful not dour.

As we've seen throughout this book, creation sets the pattern for human life and culture. God shapes space, and we form spaces within His cosmic temple. He speaks the world into being, and our social and cultural lives are ongoing, intergenerational dialogues. He divides and reunites, constructing creation by sacrificial labor, and sacrifice is at the heart of human society. He sets the world's temporal rhythms, and every culture puts its own stamp on time.

Sabbath is also an inescapable feature of culture. I don't mean that every culture observes a day of rest. They don't. Israel was unique in the ancient world, and the church has a unique weekly pattern too. But Sabbath isn't just rest. It's joy and satisfaction. It comes at the end of the creation week and is the end toward which God works.

Every culture mimics God by offering some hope for future bliss. That hope may be for the nothingness of Nirvana, an escape from suffering, or eternal life with a bevy of nubile virgins. The hopes aren't necessarily religious. Modern cultures encourage us to find our bliss in material wealth, peace of mind, an ever-expanding economy, being left alone to do our own thing. Marx dreamed about the end of social classes and the extension of individual freedom so everyone could be a manual laborer in the morning, a philosopher in the afternoon, and an artist in the evening. In practice, Marxism hasn't been so benign.

Promises of joy motivate individual and collective action. Why were so many willing to die in two World Wars? On one side, many died for a dream of world domination. On the other side, many died to protect their way of life, their freedom, their prosperity. Why do people work themselves sick with eighty-hour weeks at the office? They're seeking some joy, perhaps the joy of the work itself, perhaps the joy of a large bonus, perhaps the joy of notoriety. Alone and together, we live toward what we think will bring us to bliss.

Since Adam's sin, human hopes are distorted and perverse. Cultures inculcate joy in things that cannot bring joy. They direct our hopes to things that are finally hopeless. The liturgy exists to redirect our hopes and joys toward their proper object because the liturgy directs us to find our joy in the joy of the Lord of Sabbath. The gospel calls us into a liturgy of life that's a liturgy of joy.

Seeking Worshipers

This is one important thread of Paul's letter to the Romans: God turns idolaters into worshipers who enter His kingdom of joy.

At the outset of the epistle, Paul describes a world descending into chaos (Rom 1:18–32). Men turn their sexual desires from women to other men, and women burn with unnatural lust for other women. Their minds are darkened and depraved. People are dominated by greed, envy, violence, strife, lies, malice. They slander, boast, resent their parents, hate one another. They know God hates these things, but they keep doing them. They become so perverse that they praise those who defy God.

It's a bleak picture, but where does it start? It starts with worship. God makes Himself known in creation, but men suppress the truth. They know God but don't honor Him as God or give thanks. They know God's power and divine nature but venerate images of birds, animals, and creeping things. When men turn to idols, God gives them over to sexual confusion. When they persist in sexual perversions, God gives them over to social and moral chaos.

Corruption of the sanctuary, the place of worship, leads to corruption of the home, of marriage and sexuality. And from the sanctuary and the home, death flows out to fill the world with corruption. Sanctuary, home, world, these three. But the beginning of these is the sanctuary.

As Paul explains and expounds it in Romans, the gospel is good news about the restoration of proper worship, which reorients the home and the world. Jesus the son of David has been raised by the Spirit to become king (Rom 1:1–4). He rules to enact God's justice (Rom 1:17–18). He gives the gift of righteousness so men and women will worship His Father.

Abraham is the model. He believes God and is reckoned righteous. He believes God's promise to make him the father of nations and to give him seed through Sarah. By believing that God can call what is not as though it is, he gives "glory to God" (Rom 4:20). While the rest of the world turns to idols, Abraham is the father of worshipers because he is the father of believers.

Because of Adam's transgression, Sin and Death reign (Rom 5:12–21). By one act of obedience, Jesus triumphs over Sin and Death. Those who receive righteousness "reign in life" through Jesus (Rom 5:17).

How are you freed from sin and death? By dying and rising with Jesus in His death and resurrection, a union that occurs at baptism. Those who die in the waters of baptism are freed from the Adamic reign of Death (Rom 6:1–7). Baptism extracts us from the world of Adam and brings us into the body of Christ, the people who are united by the Spirit to the incarnate Son. Within the church, the Spirit sanctifies the baptized so that we become true worshipers. Through baptism, God releases our bodies from our slavery to injustice. Paul uses the liturgical language of "presentation" to describe what the baptized do with their bodies. Instead of dishonoring our bodies by idols and sexual sin, we "present [our] members as instruments of justice to God" (Rom 6:13). By offering our bodies in worship, we bring the justice of God to reality.

From Paul's perspective, the entire life of the Christian and of the church is liturgical (Rom 12:1-2). We are to present our bodies as living sacrifices. This, Paul says, is our "liturgy" (Greek *latreia*) guided by the word (*logike*). Christians enact the liturgy of life by using our spiritual gifts for the benefit of the whole body (Rom 12:4-8). Our liturgy is a life of love, diligence and fervor, prayer, perseverance, generosity, hospitality, unity of mind (Rom 12:9-16). If we're doing the Christian liturgy of life, we renounce vengeance. We never pay back evil for evil but overcome evil, including evil empires, with good (Rom 12:17-21; 13:1-7).

Paul describes a *corporate* liturgy, the civic liturgy of the *polis* of God. In this city, in this kingdom, what matters isn't food and drink but righteousness, peace, and joy (Rom 14:17). The gospel calls people from the darkness and chaos into the Spirit's joy. That is, it calls us from idolatrous worship into the Christian liturgy.

Joy in the Spirit

What kind of people does God want? What kind of people does the liturgy produce? The Son pours out the Spirit to bring out the fruits of the Spirit: love, joy, peace, patience, kindness, goodness, faithfulness, gentleness, self-control (Gal 5:22-23). Those fruits should characterize members of the body of Christ. Those practices set the tonality of the church's corporate life.

Joy is the most immediate and evident effect of the Spirit's advent. Filled with the Spirit, Mary rejoices in God the Savior (Luke 1:47). When the seventy return from their mission, Jesus rejoices in the Spirit (Luke 10:21). Jesus goes to the cross "for the joy that was set before Him" (Heb 12:2). After Pentecost, the disciples are "continually filled with joy and with the Holy Spirit" (Acts 13:52). The members of the church are to imitate the apostles and Jesus, clinging to the word "in much tribulation with the joy of the Holy Spirit" (1 Thess 1:6).

In every dimension, the liturgy means joy. Liturgical space is the space of joy. When Yahweh planted Israel in the land, He chose a place to set His name, where Israel would gather to "eat, drink, and rejoice" before Him (Deut 12). Joy infused the temple dedication and followed Israel as they returned to their tents (1 Kgs 8:66).

During the feasts at the sanctuary, Israel enjoyed Yahweh's blessing on their labor and the produce of their hands so they would be altogether joyful (Deut 16:15). In His presence, at His house, is the fullness of joy (Psa 16:7).

The dialogue of the liturgy is a dialogue of love between Jesus the Bridegroom and His Bride the church. It is also an ecstatic dialogue of joy. The Bridegroom rejoices over us as a mighty man over his bride and calls us to enter His joy (Zeph 3:17). The liturgy is a journey into joy. The Latin Mass begins with Psalm 43: "*Introibo ad altere dei*," and the people respond with "*Ad Deum qui laetificat juventutem meam*." "I will go to the altar of God / to God who is the joy of my youth." The Bridegroom, anointed with the oil of joy, calls the Bride to His house:

> But let all who take refuge in You be glad, let them ever sing for joy; and may You shelter them, that those who love Your name may exult in You (Psa 5:11).

> Sing for joy in the Lord, O you righteous ones; praise is becoming to the upright. . . . Sing to Him a new song; play skillfully with a shout of joy. (Psa 33:1, 3).

> O clap your hands, all peoples; shout to God with the voice of joy (Psa 47:1).

> Shout joyfully to the Lord, all the earth (Psa 100:1).

Exiled from the land, David longs to rejoin the throng in procession to the house of God so He can join his voice to the "voice of joy and gladness" of "a multitude keeping festival" (Psa 42:4). If the ministry of condemnation (2 Cor 3) came with joy, how much more the ministry of righteousness. For we have not come to another Sinai, a fearsome mountain that cannot be touched. We have come to the heavenly Zion, with its joyous assembly of angels and saints (Heb 12:18–24).

Every step in the liturgy's procession is surrounded by joy. We arrive and enter with thanksgiving and praise. We confess, and the minister pronounces absolution. In deliverance from guilt, there is joy: "Deliver me from bloodguiltiness, O God, the God of my salvation; then my tongue will joyfully sing of Your righteousness" (Psa 51:14). Confession and absolution moves us from lament to laughter, from sackcloth to song.

Having been cleansed, we ascend into heavenly places on the wings of song as we sing from the songbook of Scripture, the book of Psalms:

> Let them also offer sacrifices of thanksgiving, and tell of His works with joyful singing (Psa 107:22).

> Let Your priests be clothed with righteousness, and let Your godly ones sing for joy (Psa 132:9).

Because the Lord has rescued David from his enemies and lifted him above his enemies, he offers sacrifices in His tent "with shouts of joy" (Psa 27:6). He wants to "sing for joy" under the wings of the cherubim (Psa 63:7). The sacrifice of song is a sacrifice of joy and a sacrifice that induces joy and makes singers joyful. In the music of the church, joy compounds joy in a spiral that ascends to become a sweet sound in the ears of the Father. We sing in the Spirit, who is the Spirit of joy.

Joy is lively. Joy is active. When we rejoice, we don't

mumble or mutter. We shout and sing at the top of our lungs. When we rejoice, we move, clap, sway, dance. Joy doesn't belong down down down down in my heart. Joy grips my body, my tongue and hands and feet. Clothed in the Spirit, my body rejoices. What should liturgy look like? Don't think grim and proper Presbyterians. Think African Anglicans. Think Brazilian charismatics. Don't quench the Spirit. Don't bottle up the joy.

God speaks through Scripture and in preaching, and the church rejoices at the voice of the Shepherd because His testimonies are "the joy of my heart" (Psa 119:111). The Word of the Lord is a source of joy, more than riches or spoil after a battle (Psa 119: 14, 162).

At the peak of the mountain, God speaks to us and feeds us. His table is a table of delights, a feast of wine, and in the Bible, wine means joy. The wine of Jesus' blood offers genuine gladness, unlike the deceptive wine of the world. In the Song of Moses (Deut 32), Moses says that the vine of Israel grew from a cutting from Sodom's vine, from the vineyard of Gomorrah. Such vines produce only bitter fruit or worse—venom from dragons (*tanniyn*; vv. 32–33). Isaiah picks up the image when he complains about the worthless grapes produced by the vineyard of Jerusalem (Isa 5:1–7). Not coincidentally, Isaiah has earlier charged that Jerusalem has become Sodom (1:9–10; 3:9). The wine of Jerusalem's feasts is the poisonous wine of the serpent (cf. 5:11–12).

Always, there's wine and there's wine: There's the wine of the dragon, the serpent that poisons; and there's the wine of the One who was lifted like the Bronze Serpent, struck, and killed. Only the latter wine lifts up the heart.

Bread and wine are things, created things transformed into cultural artifacts. These things bring us joy. And bread and wine stand for all other things. We rejoice in the Lord, but that joy in the Lord takes the form of delight in His gifts, *all* His gifts.

Because we find joy in Eucharistic bread and wine, we also find joy in the plate that holds the bread and the chalice that contains the wine. We rejoice in the table and the pulpit and the windows and the paintings or banners. Dismissed from the liturgy, we go out in joy—to find joy in pots and pans, trees and flowers, mountains and sunsets, sleek cars and powerful smart phones, joy in a husband or a wife, children or siblings, friends and neighbors. We find joy in all God's gifts, which means we find joy in *everything* because we have nothing we have not received (1 Cor 4:7).

We cannot find joy in *abusing* His gifts. There's joy in sex, but no joy in adultery. There's joy in a family feast, but no joy in a house full of bickering, back-biting, and strife. There's joy in material goods, but no joy in greed or a life devoted to Mammon.

After eating, the church is sent out. The Bride rejoices in the presence of the Bridegroom, and she goes out rejoicing, to spread joy to the whole earth. Nations are called to join the joyful assembly (Psa 66:1; 67:4), and even creation is summoned to join in (Psa 65:13). The church's mission is to live joyfully, inviting the world into joy.

We enter with joy, receive forgiveness with joy, ascend with joy, hear with joy, feast with joy, depart in joy. The liturgy welcomes the sad, sad world and leads it to the joy of God. The liturgy confronts the false and fruitless joys of the world and reorients them to the One in whom there is fullness of joy. Cultures always aim at joy but miss their target. Over decades and centuries, the liturgy redeems culture by redirecting its quest for bliss. Liturgy redeems because it's a culture of joy.

As I've emphasized again and again, there's no magic here. The liturgy doesn't *automatically* bring true joy. In some churches, the liturgy is quite joyless. And we can't expect to thrill in the Spirit's joy unless we are walking in the Spirit. A quenched Spirit, a grieved Spirit, doesn't elicit joy but rather witnesses against us, convicting us, along with the world of sin, righteousness, and judgment. If we want the liturgy to be a journey to joy, the church and each member must trust and obey the Lord who is Spirit.

Joy in Sorrow

All this joy may strike you as Pollyannish or even cruel. What right does the church have to rejoice in a world of sex abuse and slavery, hunger and homelessness, sorrow and terror and cruelty? How *dare* we?

Christian joy doesn't ignore the evils of the world or the anguish of existence. Christians, after all, follow a crucified Lord, who instructs us to take up our own crosses to follow Him. Jesus experienced the full range of weakness and woe.

But here's God's commitment to His people: Sorrow *never* has the last word. Darkness *never* triumphs over light. The light comes into the world, and darkness *cannot* overcome it. After darkness, light. After the grave, resurrection.

This is one of the key lessons we learn by singing the Psalms of lament. They begin with the most poignant descriptions of human pain ever written. David is driven from his home. He suffers physical deprivations and pain. His friends betray him, and, worst of all, it seems Yahweh has abandoned him. Before the end of the Psalm, the mood turns. David remembers the Lord's promise. He may not yet be delivered, but he's certain he will be. Yahweh's promise is enough. He prepares a table in the midst of enemies (Psa 23:5), assuring David he will look in triumph on his foes (Psa 59:10).

Singing the Psalms, we sing the Lord's promises of joy. Even in the *midst* of sorrow, we rejoice in the coming joy. The very fact that Jesus enters our sorrows transforms our sorrows. The Good Shepherd is with us in the valley of the shadow. Jesus is Lord of the grave so that whether we live *or* die, we are the Lord's. Jesus went to the cross for the joy set before Him. But more: The cross is the beginning of His ascent to the Father. It's the first step in His journey to joy. Joy comes at the end, but the light of the destination shines on the path.

And so it is in the liturgy. The liturgy gives us a taste now of the kingdom to come. In the liturgy, we glimpse endless day. In the liturgy, we experience now the joy of resurrection and the eternal marriage feast of the Lamb. We gather with broken relationships, failed hopes, frustrated dreams. We don't leave behind our sorrows any more than we leave behind our language and culture. As the liturgy transforms our language and culture, so it brings our sorrows into the joy of the Spirit.

Joyous Mission

So the liturgy is joyful. Liturgical culture is joyful culture. But *so what*? What does that have to do with anything? How does *joy* advance the mission of the church? How does a joyful liturgy in the city of God transform the city of man?

Let's start with a baseline answer: The city of God isn't merely a city of moral uprightness. The liturgy doesn't aim to form merely "virtuous" people. Obsession with the minutiae of law is Pharisaical, not Christian. The church can build a "Christian" culture that's an empty shell. All the forms and patterns are right, but there's no life.

Joylessness is a mark of deep trouble. If a community is Christian, it must be enlivened by the fruits of the Spirit. If a culture is transformed by the church's ministry in the Spirit, it must manifest the work of the Spirit. Where the Spirit is, there is joy, and the faith of joyous Christians is contagious.

For Western Christians, there's a contextual reason to emphasize joy. Nietzsche complained Christians have no joy. We shouldn't dismiss this comment just because Nietzsche was an enemy of the church. To the extent it's true, it's a fundamental indictment. If the Spirit brings joy, a joyless church must be Ichabod, bereft of the Spirit of glory and joy.

Outside the church, many are desperate. Life is stale, flat, unprofitable, meaningless. Nothing delights. Nothing causes wonder. It's same old, same old, same old, till the last syllable of recorded time. We can identify various causes for the ennui of the contemporary mood. We're over-saturated with stimulation. Technology is partly to blame. We've lost confidence in institutions. We have no heroes. We cynically think everyone's on the make.

At heart, though, the joylessness of modern life reflects the joylessness of the church. The church is the light of the world, radiating the light of Jesus by the Spirit among the nations. The church is the place of joy; the liturgy is the time of joy. If there is no joy at the center, there will be none at the edges. If there's no joy in the sanctuary, no joy will flow out. If the redeemed culture of the liturgy isn't joyous, nothing will be.

The Lord's Service

Joy is a gift of the Spirit. The liturgy is a journey to joy because it's the Spirit's work. From beginning to end, the liturgy is God's work in and for us.

God always initiates worship. He calls us into His presence, a place where we wouldn't dare go without an invitation. Every worship service should begin with an acknowledgement that He gets things rolling. Every worship service should begin with a call to worship, an invocation of His name: "In the Name of God the Father, God the Son, and God the Holy Spirit." With this summons, the minister also names our destination because our liturgical journey is a journey into the Triune life, the communion of eternal joy.

If we stop there, we've misunderstood the liturgy. Liturgy isn't Deist. It's not that God kicks things off and then leaves us to muster up the strength for the rest of the work. God is the primary actor throughout the liturgy, from start to finish. *He* calls us into His house. *He* forgives us. *He* speaks to us. *He* feeds us. He feeds Himself to us, as the Father gives the body and blood of the Son through the Spirit.

The liturgy is primarily God's action, not ours. No wonder it's a time for rejoicing.

That's true in an obvious way. Ever since Adam honored the serpent above God, we've all been idolaters, worshiping and serving the creature rather than the Creator (Rom 1). We worship rightly only because the Spirit turns us from idols to the living God. The liturgy is utterly dependent on God's work *in* us.

But the liturgy is also God's work *for* us and *towards* us. The liturgy is the Lord's service, not primarily because we serve Him but because in the liturgy *He serves us*.

This is true under the law, though God parcels out His gifts less lavishly. Think about Israel's worship. They're permitted to enter the courtyard of the sanctuary but can't enter the Holy Place, where there's bread, light, and incense. The priests can enter the Holy Place, but even they're excluded from the Most Holy Place, God's throne room.

The ark of the covenant is the one piece of furniture in the Most Holy Place (Exod 25:10–22). At the top of the ark is the cherubim throne of Yahweh, where He sits above the wings. Beneath the throne is a box, covered inside and outside with gold, a treasure chest. In the treasure chest are the tablets of the law, inscribed by the Spirit-finger of God; a jar of manna; and the staff of Aaron that budded and blossomed (Heb 9:4).

These are God's treasures, the treasures King Yahweh offers to His people: the bread of life, the wisdom of Torah, the guidance of a priest—food, word, and a shepherd. All these treasures are under the Lord's throne, but no one can go in to get them. Not the lay Israelite, not the priest, not even the high priest. Yahweh's treasures are locked away in His inner vault.

Until...

Until Jesus comes. Jesus offers Himself as a final sacrifice. He passes through death to resurrection life. He goes behind the veil into the throne room. He passes through the firmament and enters the original sanctuary, the heavenly one (Heb 9:11–22; 10:19–22). He isn't a suppliant approaching the throne. He's the Conqueror, who takes the throne.

Jesus isn't descended from Aaron. He's from the tribe of Judah, not Levi. He's not qualified to enter the earthly temple. But He *is* a priest. He's a priest after the order of Melchizedek, qualified not by fleshly descent but by resurrection (Heb 7).

As a priest in the Melchizedekan order, Jesus enters a better sanctuary, the heavenly one. He doesn't come in through the blood of an animal; He sprinkles His own blood. He doesn't have to offer sacrifices again and again; He offers Himself, the sacrifice of complete obedience, once and for all.

Jesus doesn't stop His priestly work with His death on the cross. Jesus doesn't stop being Priest when He rises again, or ascends. He "ever lives" as priest, to make intercession, to lead us in worship, to be the chief singer of the choir of God (Heb 7:25).

Now, at last, there's a priest who won't stop being priest because He can't die. Now, at last, there's a sanctuary that won't be dismantled or move away because it's safe in heaven. And now, at last, we can receive the treasures God has stored up for us in His house. Having ascended on high, Jesus gives gifts to men (Eph 4:7–13), distributed through the Spirit, who equips the members of the church with gifts to edify the entire body.

Through the Spirit, we receive the true manna from heaven,

the body and blood of the Lord Jesus. Through the Spirit, God speaks His word and so reveals His living Word. Through the Spirit, the minister guides us with the rod and staff of the Good Shepherd. Through the Spirit, He gives life, wisdom, and glory.

This is what happens in the Christian liturgy. We're no longer at a distance, out in the court. We gather in the throne room. Jesus is with us by His Spirit, and Jesus gives away His gifts. He girds Himself as He did in the upper room, and *He* serves *us*. Through the Spirit, He gives the gift of bread, the gift of word, the gift of a shepherd. In, with, and under all these gifts, the Spirit gives us the gift of joy. Food, word, shepherd: These gifts are joy incarnate.

Am I waxing mystical? In a sense, yes. Since God is active in the liturgy, there are things happening we can't explain. There's a kind of liturgical magic as the Lord takes up our places, our words, our sacrifices, our time-keeping and transforms them into anticipations of the heavenly city.

Culture isn't Christianized in the liturgy by some sociological process or ministerial manipulations. It's Christianized because it's touched by the magical finger of God.

Still, we can think about it concretely. If you were an Israelite in the temple courts, you'd never see bread set out on the table of showbread, much less manna from the ark. You'd never see the lampstand, much less the tablets of the law. You might glimpse some priests, but they'd keep disappearing through the veil and then reappearing.

Now, what do you see when you enter church? Okay, what *should* you see? There's a Bible up on a lectern—the completed word. Bread and wine are laid out on the table—manna. There's a man wearing a white robe at the front, leading worship—the pastor-shepherd. That can mean only one thing: You're *in*! You've entered the heavenly Most Holy Place. You're inside the ark of God.

What you *shouldn't* see is a barrier between you and the Bible. You shouldn't see a rail dividing the Lord's table from the congregation. You shouldn't see anything that sends the message you're on the outside. Because you're *not*. You're as far inside as you can get. You're in the throne room, and your Father is there with His Son and Spirit, to feed you, to speak to you, to guide you through the valley of the shadow.

You aren't just inside an earthly sanctuary. By the Spirit, heaven and earth join in the liturgy. You don't come to Sinai any more, with all its thunders and terrors. You *have* come—not will, but *have*—to another mountain, to the heavenly Zion (Heb 12:18–24). When you enter the church building, you're entering heaven. That's where the liturgy takes us, right into the throne room, into the presence of eternal joy.

This is at the heart of the good news of Jesus. The gospel announces Jesus the priest has entered the heavenly sanctuary and opened up a way for us to follow. The good news is that all the treasure of the throne room is distributed freely to Jesus' loyal disciples. The gospel is the good news of an open sanctuary. The gospel is an inherently *liturgical* gospel and so is inherently a gospel of joy.

You might be thinking, "Are you saying we go to church to *get* something from God? I thought we were supposed to *give* something to Him—praise, honor, glory. I thought worship was supposed to be *God*-centered."

If you're thinking that, you're catching the drift. That's just what I'm saying: We gather in the presence of God to *receive* His treasures. We go to church because of what we can *get* there. We gather in His presence because we want Him to share His joy.

Of course, there's a bad way to "go to get." If you go to church to get an emotional high, that's not healthy. If you go to church to have an experience, you're likely to be tossed around by your emotions. If you go to church because you think it's socially advantageous, you must be living in the 1950s.

But think about it: Do you *really* think that you have something to give to God? *Really*? If so, repent. You *don't*. You have nothing you haven't received. You have nothing He needs. Outside of church, we know that we can't do anything without God's grace. We can't believe, obey, trust, love, display the fruits of the Spirit without the Spirit's work in us. Let's stop being pious. Let's be real: You can't breathe, digest, urinate, defecate, or pump blood through your veins without the power of the Spirit.

Somehow, when we enter the church building, we become giddy Pelagians who think we can muster up something from our own riches. We think that we can bring treasures of our own and present them to God.

We *do* present ourselves as sacrifices (see chapter 3). But we do that only as a response to His gifts and treasures. That response is *itself* a gift. The liturgy is just like everything else: We give only because we have first received. We love because He first loved us. We rejoice because we receive joy.

That's God-centeredness, a proper God-centeredness, a *Triune* God-centeredness. The Triune God isn't glorified by keeping glory to Himself. The Father is glorified as He glorifies the Son in the Spirit, and the Son is lifted up by honoring the Father through the Spirit. We are properly God-centered, *Triunely* God-centered, when we receive the treasures He offers, when we accept the glory and joy of the Father so that we might glorify and delight Him and share His glory and joy with the world. We gather for the liturgy in order to receive the Father's gifted Spirit, who is the gift of joy.

EPILOGUE

What have we discovered?

We've discovered things about creation. Creation is a temple. Life is a dialogue. History moves in a sacrificial pattern of death and renewal. God created timekeepers to mark the appointed times when we enter the joy of the Bridegroom.

We've learned where creation is headed. One day, the new heavens and earth will be a civic temple, the heavenly Jerusalem. Life is dialogue, and one day we will all be Moses, who speaks to Yahweh mouth-to-mouth. The dialogue of history will be fulfilled in the Bridegroom's eternal kiss. One day, the sacrificial pattern of death and renewal will give way to endless life. One day, sun and moon will fade before the glory of God and the Lamb. One day, there will be joy, only joy, to ages of ages.

To say all that is to say *creation* is liturgical all the way down. To say all that is to say God moves creation toward a liturgical consummation.

We've learned things about culture too. Culture inescapably moves in the liturgical grooves of creation. Mimicking the divine architect, we build and adorn places within the place of creation. Made in the image of the Word, we carry on a dialogue within the cosmic dialogue between Creator and creation. Human history replicates the sacrificial movements of creation, and political communities are founded on and for sacrifice. We give communal shape to the created rhythms of time, setting aside moments to eat, drink, and rejoice.

To say all of this is to say that *culture* is inherently liturgical.

Teach me how you build, how you speak, what you will die and kill for. Show me your calendar and tell me the wellspring of your joy. Teach me this, and I will learn your culture. That is: Teach me your liturgy, so I can sing and sway along.

Liturgy crystallizes culture. Culture is the flowering of liturgy. Culture is liturgy stretched out into life. Culture is the liturgy of everyday life.

Culture is the bridge between beginning and end. God created a good but unfinished world and made us as His images to finish it. Through our building, speech, sacrifice, timekeeping, and joy, we glorify the creation. Through our cultural labors, creation moves toward consummation. Through *us*, the Spirit broods over the dark abyss and calls it into light.

We've learned things about the effects of sin. Since Adam sinned and brought death into the world, cultures have run at cross-purposes to the Creator and His creation. We build and adorn shrines to idols—Zeus and Molech, but also France and America and Mother Russia. We build to keep Untouchables and African Americans on the other side of the tracks. Our built culture, our organization of space, offends God. It doesn't glorify but perverts the good creation.

Human lies replace God's truth. Tyrants hard and soft force their subjects to immolate themselves to brute and mute idols of blood and soil and the Proletariat. Liberals and dictators rule time without honoring Jesus, Lord of ages. We're dazzled by the works of our hands and are seduced into seeking our joy in them.

Since Adam's sin, all the created patterns of culture—place, language, sacrifice, time, joy—are twisted. If there's going to be a cultural bridge from creation to consummation, culture has to be put right. Unless something is done, the liturgy of creation will dissolve into a formless void or a temple of terrors.

The gospel announces that something *has* been done. The Father sent the Son to live, die, rise, and ascend to harmonize culture with creation and the Creator and to direct it toward glory. The Father and Son poured out the Spirit to reestablish the created fit between God's works and ours. The liturgy is the Spirit's work to accomplish that mission.

Creation's liturgy stretches toward liturgical consummation. Human culture bridges the time between. But culture is a bridge from Jerusalem now to Jerusalem not yet only when it's purged and transfigured by incorporation into the divine service. A biblically-formed liturgy done by Spirit-filled and Spirit-led disciples *is* the first redemption of culture.

Specifically:

- *Place*: Creation is a temple, designed to grow from glory to glory until it becomes new Jerusalem. When we build a church for the worship of God, we're turning creation to its intended end. A gathered church, a church building that is a cultural product, anticipates the fulfillment of creation in the eschaton.
- *Dialogue*: Language exists so God can speak to us and we can speak back. It exists so we can speak to one another in God, and speak from generation to generation. The liturgy uses language as it's designed to be used. It calls us into dialogue with the primary Speaker, which renews our speech to Him and one another.
- *Sacrifice*: The sacrifice of praise unmasks the pretense of liberalism to live beyond sacrifice and subverts the violent sacrifices of ancient and modern despotisms. In the

liturgy, we offer true human sacrifice, so that we may offer ourselves as witnesses in daily sacrifice.
- *Time*: God created the heavens as a liturgical clock, but Adam's children put time out of joint. The liturgy re-orders our time, so our time-keeping is shaped by the life, death, resurrection, and ascension of Jesus, stamped with the rhythms of Triune life.
- *Joy*: At the end of creation week, God enters into His joy and intends to invite us to share His joy. After Adam, we pursue false joys and pleasures. In the liturgy, we're re-directed from counterfeit joys into the delights of God, so that we can enjoy the creation as God's gift.

Liturgy doesn't stand outside the world. It takes place in the world. Or, better, the world, the true world and the new world, takes place and takes form in the liturgy. Liturgy transforms the world as it takes up creation and culture so they become a foretaste of the kingdom.

FOR FURTHER READING

Branch, Lori. *Rituals of Spontaneity: Sentiment and Secularism from Free Prayer to Wordsworth.* Waco, TX: Baylor University Press, 2006.

Gallant, Tim. *Feed My Lambs.* Grande Prairie, Alberta: Pactum Books, 2001.

Johnson, Dru. *Human Rites: The Power of Rituals, Habits, and Sacraments.* Grand Rapids: Eerdmans, 2019.

Jordan, James B. *Liturgical Nestorianism.* Niceville, FL: Transfiguration Press, 1994.

Jordan, James B. *Theses on Worship: Notes Toward the Reformation of Worship.* Niceville, FL: Transfiguration Press, 1998.

Leithart, Peter J. *Daddy, Why Was I Excommunicated?* Niceville, FL: Transfiguration Press, 1998.

Leithart, Peter J. *Blessed Are the Hungry: Meditations on the Lord's Supper.* Moscow, ID: Canon Press, 2000.

Leithart, Peter J. *From Silence to Song: The Davidic Liturgical Revolution.* Moscow, ID: Canon Press, 2003.

Leithart, Peter J. *The Baptized Body*. Moscow, ID: Canon Press, 2007.

Leithart, Peter J. *The Theopolitan Vision*. Monroe, LA: Theopolis Books, 2019.

Meyers, Jeffrey J. *The Lord's Service: The Grace of Covenant Renewal Worship*. Moscow, ID: Canon Press, 2003.

Page, Christopher. *The Christian West and Its Singers: The First Thousand Years*. New Haven: Yale University Press, 2010.

Schmemann, Alexander. *For the Life of the World*. Crestwood, NY: St. Vladimir's Seminary Press, 2018.

Smith, James K.A. *You Are What You Love: The Spiritual Power of Habit*. Grand Rapids: Brazos Press, 2016.

Strawbridge, Gregg, ed. *The Case for Covenantal Infant Baptism*. Phillipsburg, NJ: P&R Publishing, 2003.

Thompson, Bard. *Liturgies of the Western Church*. Eastford, CT: Martino Fine Books, 2015.

www.ingramcontent.com/pod-product-compliance
Lightning Source LLC
Chambersburg PA
CBHW060452080526
44584CB00015B/1411